Complete Crochet

Complete
Crochet

Techniques & Projects

First Published in North America in 2006 by

CRE▲TIVE
HOMEOWNER®

Creative Homeowner® is a registered trademark of Federal Marketing Corporation

International Standard Book Number : 1-58011-294-3
Library of Congress Catalog Card Number: 2006929854

Current printing (last digit)
10 9 8 7 6 5 4 3 2 1

Produced by Collins & Brown
151 Freston Road
London
W10 6TH

An imprint of Anova Books Company Ltd

Commissioning Editor: Michelle Lo
Design Manager: Gemma Wilson
Editor: Marie Clayton
Photographer: Mark Winwood
Crochet Designers: Sophie Britten, Luise Roberts, Sue Whiting
Designer: Ben Kracknell Studios
Production Controller: Laura Brodie
Editorial Assistant: Katie Hudson

Printed and bound in WKT Co Ltd, China

CREATIVE HOMEOWNER
A Division of Federal Marketing Corp.
24 Park Way
Upper Saddle River, NJ 07458

www.creativehomeowner.com

Contents

Introduction

Many years ago, crochet was something that grandmothers did to use up oddments of yarn—they created granny square afghans in bright colors or endless doilies to decorate dressing tables and sideboards. However, crochet has recently experienced a quiet revolution—funky Italian designers have included crochet garments and accessories in their catwalk collections, and these days every fashion-conscious person needs to know how to crochet.

The basics of crochet are really simple—you just need to know how to make a chain and then how to work single, half-double, double and treble stitch. These stitches are all carried out in the same way—the only variation is in the number of times you wrap the yarn over the hook and therefore the number of loops you pull through the loop on the hook. Once you have mastered these stitches, you will have learned the basics to create almost any pattern, and with the addition of other simple skills to add and decrease stitches, a couple of decorative techniques—and a little bit of practice—you will soon be able to crochet almost anything.

Another great thing about crochet is that it is very portable. Unlike some other crafts, it does not require space, lots of special tools or access to water or electricity. You really can work almost anywhere—at home, on the beach, waiting in a line! Most large projects are made up of smaller units, so you can carry your work around to do whenever you have a spare minute. If you need to leave it for some time, it will still be there, in the same condition, waiting to be picked up and completed. It's the ideal craft for a busy person—you can devote as much or as little time as you choose.

The joy of creating your own crocheted item is that it really can be unique to you. The designer creates the pattern, but even if you follow it exactly, you can still choose a different color yarn and make something that does not look exactly like the same item made by someone else. When you have a little skill and confidence you can customize even more—substitute a different edging, for instance, or change a fringe for bobbles or a lacy trim. Crochet can also be added to shop-bought garments—a pretty crochet edging worked onto the hem or cuffs of a plain sweater will make it totally unique.

At the back of this book, you will find 25 diverse and exciting projects by designers Sophie Britten, Luise Roberts, and Sue Whiting to get you started. They include accessories, clothes, projects for the home and items for babies and children, suitable for a range of skill levels. Expand your wardrobe with the glamorous silk Tank Top, make the Pendant Bead Necklace to dress up a plain outfit or amuse the little one in your life with the adorable Floppy Rabbit. Crochet is fun, it's versatile and it's addictive. Pick up your hook and yarn, grab this book, and off you go.

Getting Started

Crochet is a relatively simple craft to learn. It's comprised of a series of interlocking loops where each stitch is completed before working the next. It's so easy, you'll be hooked in no time!

Equipment

Just a few, inexpensive pieces of equipment are required for crochet. Most you may already have, and hooks can be acquired gradually as the need for them arises.

Hooks

Crochet hooks are mostly found in aluminum, but are also available in plastic, bamboo, or wood—particularly the larger sizes. Whatever material they are made of, hooks are sized using a standard system—but there are three different systems, all of which are widely recognized, so one or more will be quoted in most crochet patterns. The US has its own system, Europe and the UK use a metric system, and there are also still hooks sized using an old UK and Canadian system. The Hook Conversion chart opposite gives some idea of equivalent sizes between these three systems, but the conversions cannot be exact as the sizes are calculated in different ways—you may well find slightly different equivalent sizes in other sources! It can be a matter of trial and error until you get the gauge you need. There is a different set of sizes for the very fine steel hooks, which are used when working with cotton threads.

Hook Conversion Chart

U.S. size	Metric	Old UK/Canadian size
–	2.00	14
B/1	2.25	13
–	2.50	12
C/2	2.75	–
–	3.00	11
D/3	3.25	10
E/4	3.50	9
F/5	3.75	–
6	4.00	8
7	4.50	7
H/8	5.00	6
I/9	5.50	5
J/10	6.00	4
K10½	6.50	3
11	7.00	2
L/12	8.00	0
M/13	9.00	00
N/15	10.00	000
P/16	16.00	–
S	19.00	–

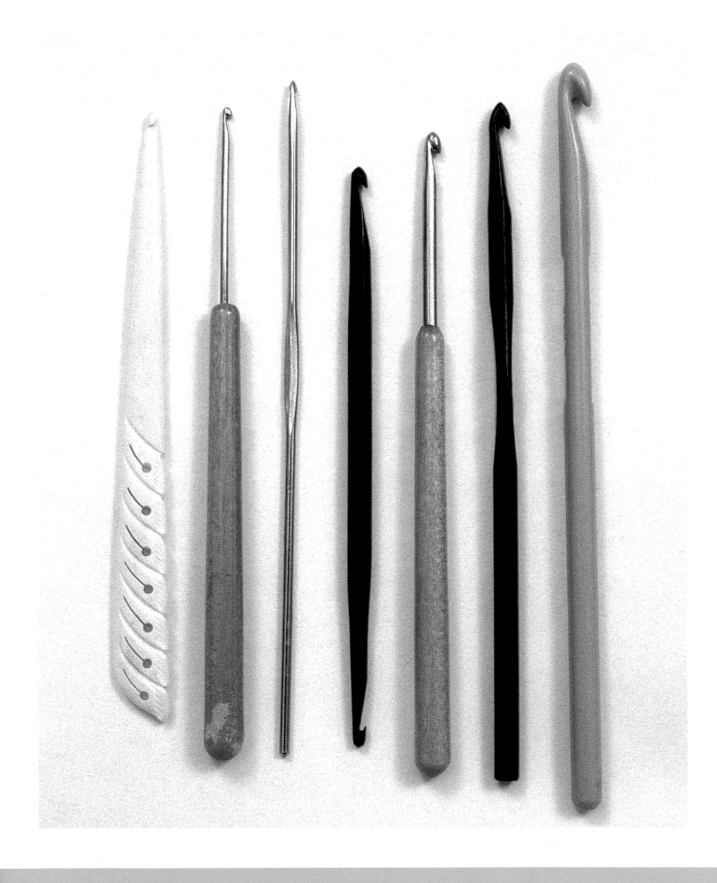

Other basic equipment

You will also find the following inexpensive pieces of equipment very useful and many of them will be in your needlework box already.

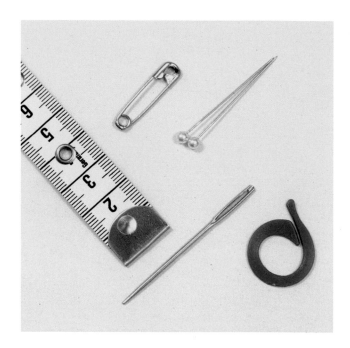

Tape measure—used to measure the gauge square and also the dimensions of the crocheted fabric as you work. Fabric tapes can stretch with age, making measurements inaccurate, so check regularly and buy a new one if necessary. Where dimensions are critical—when measuring a gauge swatch, for instance—it may be better to use a metal rule if you have one. Choose a tape measure with both imperial (inches) and metric measurements, so you do not have to bother with conversions no matter how the dimensions are given in the pattern.

Scissors—a small, sharp pair of scissors are useful to snip yarn. Choose a pair with long points rather than rounded tips to the blades as this will make it easier to separate out just one strand of yarn. Keep your needlework scissors away from other scissors and never use them to cut paper, as this can blunt the blades.

Dressmaker's pins—these are used to hold pieces of crochet together for sewing, for marking off stitches and rows in a gauge swatch, and for pinning pieces out for blocking or pressing. Choose long pins with colored heads so it will be easier to see them in the crocheted fabric.

Row counter—a small cylindrical device with a dial used to record the number of rows or rounds when this is critical, as when increasing or decreasing. However, you must remember to turn the dial at the end of each row or round. Some people prefer to mark the start with a scrap of colored yarn.

Split ring markers—these are little clips that can be attached to a piece of crochet to mark the beginning of a round, or for marking points in a stitch pattern. Again, some people prefer to use a scrap of contrasting yarn threaded through the fabric instead.

Safety pins—a selection of large safety pins are useful to hold small numbers of stitches, as markers instead of the split ring, and to roughly hold pieces together to check the dimensions are correct before sewing up.

Tapestry or yarn needle—this type of needle has a blunt point so it will not split or snag the yarn. It is used for sewing seams and needs to have an eye large enough to thread the yarn.

Yarns

Yarn is the general term used for strands of fiber that are twisted together into a continuous thread. It covers both natural fibers, such as wool, cotton, and silk, and synthetic ones such as nylon, viscose, or acrylic. It also covers varying thicknesses and both smooth and textured finishes. Synthetic yarns are strong, hardwearing, and easy to wash, but they often lack some of the fine qualities of natural yarns.

Most yarns are categorized according to the number or strands, or plies, they are made up of and by weight. Generally, the lower the ply the thinner the yarn and the lighter the final garment will be. However, yarns in the same ply are not necessarily identical. See yarnstandards.com for more information on yarn weights.

Cotton—This is the traditional yarn used for crochet and is available in a wide range of colors. Rather than being rated by ply, cotton crochet yarn comes in sizes normally ranging from 10–70, with the larger sizes denoting finer thread.

4-ply—This lightweight yarn works well for most crochet projects and is available in a wide range of colors and finishes.

Double Knitting or DK—This is one of the most popular of the standard yarns and is suitable for most crochet garments.

Aran—This yarn was traditionally cream in color and used for classic Aran designs, but is now available in a range of shades.

Worsted—This yarn can be used for crochet with the appropriately size hook.

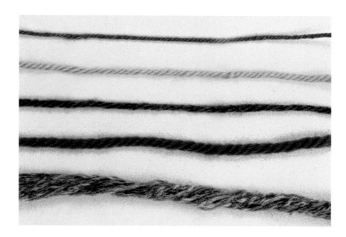

Fiber Facts

Crochet can be worked with unusual yarns, so don't be afraid to experiment. You can even use strips of fabric—see the Easy Urban Carryall on page 120!

Fluffy or hairy yarns will hide the structure of the stitch, so they are very forgiving for a beginner.

When working with textured yarns, try sitting with the light in front of you so it shines through your work and you can see where to insert the hook.

Synthetic yarns often stretch easily, so it is best to avoid them until you are more confident and are achieving an even gauge in your work.

Yarn labeling

Yarn is usually sold in balls or skeins. The company normally brands its yarn with a ball band or label that contains invaluable information about the yarn. Always keep the ball bands for reference purposes— it gives you dye lots, quantities, care instructions, and so on.

Needle sizes
Recommended knitting and crochet needle size. You may need to use a different needle size, depending on your tension/gauge.

Tension/gauge square
Ideal tension/gauge of the yarn to achieve the best performance.

Shade
Usually represented by a number.

Dye lot
Batch number of the yarn.

SHADE 8308

100% COTTON

50g (85m)

LOT 348

BRAND NAME

Cotton DK

4 x 4in
10 x 10cm
24 st
30 rows
4mm
US 6
8UK
4mm
9UK F US
40

Composition of the yarn

Weight and length

Brand name
Name of the company and of the yarn. Sometimes the company may also indicate the weight of the yarn, such as double knitting, or the standard size according to the Craft Yarn Council of America (CYCA).

Washing instructions
Recommended aftercare advice.

Choosing yarn

When learning to crochet, it is especially important to choose a yarn that feels comfortable in your hands— one that is slightly elastic and neither slippery nor so highly textured that it will not move smoothly through your fingers. Patterns normally specify exactly which brand of yarn to be used for a project. You can often substitute a different yarn for the one specified, providing that you can obtain the same gauge (see page 25). In fact you can crochet with almost any yarn you like as long as your hook is large enough. Check the length of yarn in the ball, as different types and brands have differing lengths— the length will be given on the ball band. If the length in the ball varies significantly from that of the specified yarn, you may need more or less balls to complete the item. Always buy an extra ball of yarn anyway—if you do need a bit more later the same dye match may not be available, but you can always use up extra yarn in another small project.

Ball band

The ball band gives useful information about the yarn, including the content—for instance, it may state 100% wool or 80% wool/20% angora—and washing and pressing instructions. It also gives the approximate length of yarn within the ball, which is useful if you plan to substitute a different yarn; a 50g ball of pure cotton will contain less yarn than the same weight ball of pure wool, for instance.

Fastenings

It is a good idea to consider the fastenings you may need for your garment when you buy the yarn. Most yarn stores also carry a range of fastenings, and it will be quicker and easier to match the color of buttons or zippers at the same time.

Buttons—these are made in many materials, including plastic, ceramic, glass, and wood. Make sure they are washable if the garment itself is to be washable, otherwise you will have to remove the buttons each time you want to clean it. Consider the style of the garment when choosing buttons—small pearl ones look best on a lacy garment, while big chunky ones usually work best on a larger scale outdoor garment. You will need your buttons on hand as you make the buttonholes so you can check if they fit after making the first one. If not, you will either have to remake it or choose a slightly different size of button.

Zipper—if you cannot get a zipper in the exact shade to match your yarn, choose one a little darker rather than lighter. If you have the zipper before you start crocheting, you can adjust the length of the garment to match it, if necessary.

Hook and eyes—these are usually used as a concealed fastening and they come in a wide range of sizes.

Snaps—also an invisible fastening, but will not hold under a heavy strain. Useful on garments for young children, as they may find snaps easier to use than buttons or hooks.

Fasten Times

Many of the projects in this book either don't have any fastenings or just have very simple ties or snaps—but you can always choose a different fastening if you prefer.

Remember that buttons and zippers do not have to blend in with your project, nor do they have to be purely functional—they can be made into eye-catching features.

Hook-and-loop tape is a convenient fastening but it is not ideal for crochet items as when unfastened, the hook section will easily snag on the yarn and may end up pulling threads.

Patterns

Each pattern gives a range of information at the beginning that will help you crochet the item as its designer intended it to be.

Sizing

Most patterns will give the size or sizes it is designed for at the beginning, often with a set of actual measurements as well. The actual measurements for a particular size may vary quite a bit in patterns from different designers or for different yarns, so it is always worth checking them against a ready-made garment with a good fit.

Equipment

This section gives the size of hooks and any other equipment you will need to complete the garment, although basic tools, such as tape measure, scissors, or pins will not be included. The pattern will also state the required quantity of a specified yarn and any fastenings or decorative bits that will be needed.

Gauge

The gauge required for the pattern will be expressed in number of rows and stitches you need to achieve in a 4 in. (10 cm) square, when crocheted in the stitch used for the item. To produce an item as the designer intended, you need to crochet to the same gauge. If you do not, the measurements will not come out the same, so it is important that you make a swatch to check your gauge before you begin. If you work to a different gauge you can change the size of hook you use to adjust it—for instructions on how to make a gauge swatch, see page 25.

Abbreviations

Standard crochet abbreviations are given in this book on page 171, but if the pattern has any special instructions, they will be written out in full at the start, along with the abbreviation used in the pattern.

Pattern Repeats

Most stitch patterns, unless they are completely random or worked in panels, are made up of a set of stitches that are repeated across the row, and a number of rows that are repeated throughout the length of the fabric. A pattern repeat within crochet instructions is contained within either brackets or parentheses, or follows an asterisk (*). The extra stitches outside the brackets or before the asterisk are to balance the pattern within the piece of crochet.

Pattern Play

Always read the pattern through carefully before you begin, even before you buy the yarn. You may find something you want to change—such as making the sleeves or body longer—that may affect what you finally need to buy.

When you gain in confidence, don't be afraid to experiment with the pattern. Try one of the different edgings on pages 168 to 169, or substitute a different motif for the one in the pattern.

Charts

Some patterns include charts, either showing you the placement of stitches or how to piece motifs together. When you understand them, charts are very easy to follow because they give you a pictorial version of what the design should look like.

Crochet patterns do not use charts very often, unless they are filet crochet designs or contain a complex stitch pattern. Filet crochet is based on a simple combination of either chain or double crochet, which produce either a space or a block respectively. Filet designs are drawn out on a squared grid, as shown right, with the resulting crochet design seen bottom right. It is easy to design shapes or lettering on graph paper. For more detail on filet, see page 45.

Another type of diagram, as seen below, shows the placement of different squares in a scarf with repeats of the same motif in different colorways and sizes.

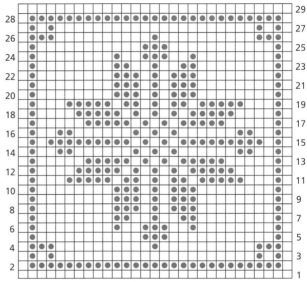

29 squares

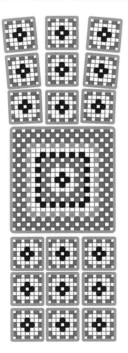

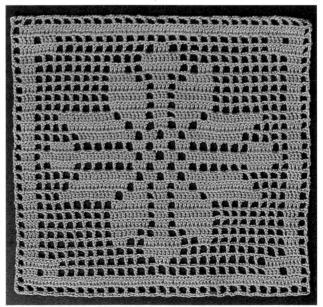

Basic Techniques

Before casting on stitches, you must get used to the hook and yarn.
At first, they might seem awkward to hold, but practice will soon make them familiar.
Just keep trying until you gain in confidence and speed.

Holding the hook

Everyone has their own way of holding the hook, so if you have found one that works for you, don't change it. The most important thing is to hold it gently and to feel comfortable.

How to hold the hook

Many crocheters hold the hook as if it were a pencil, so both the wrist and the fingers can be used to manipulate it. The thumb and forefinger go on the flat portion of the hook to give the correct balance.

Holding the yarn

The other hand holds the work and controls the yarn supply. Again, there are several different methods, so you need to experiment to find the one that suits you. The yarn must be threaded through your fingers so that it is fed evenly under tension.

How to hold the yarn

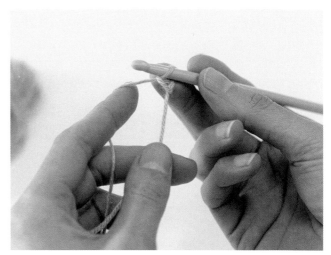

Take the yarn over the first three fingers and wrap it around the little finger. The middle finger is held above to keep the yarn taut and ready for hooking.

Making a Slip Knot

A slip knot is used to attach the yarn to the hook and
acts as a starting point for making a foundation chain.

How to make a slip knot

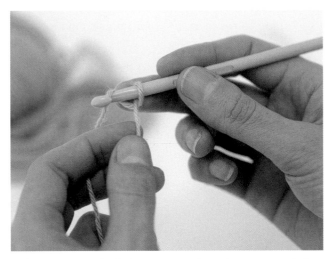

1 At the end of the yarn, make a loop around the hook.

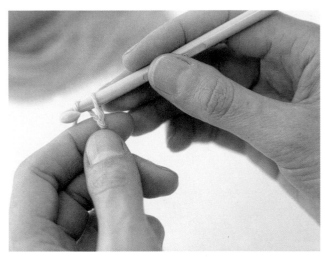

2 Catch the yarn towards the ball end with the hook.

Off the Hook!
Practice all the basic stitches on the next few pages again and again until you can work them smoothly and evenly without effort.

Learning to crochet with a smooth yarn will make it much easier for you to see the structure of the stitches, which will help you understand them and make it easier to see if you have gone wrong.

At both the beginning and the completion of every crochet stitch there should only be one loop left on your hook.

3 Pull the yarn through the loop and onto the hook.

Basic Stitches

From making a chain stitch and a slip stitch to creating
a chain ring, mastering these basic skills will establish your foundations.
All crochet stitches are built on these basic ones.

Chain stitch

Yarn over is the term used to describe the basic action used to form a crochet chain, although usually the yarn is held taut, while the hook is moved under and over it. The chain itself is a series of loops and the foundation for almost all the other crochet stitches.

Making a chain

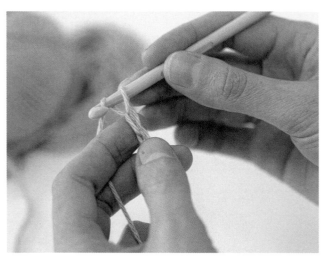

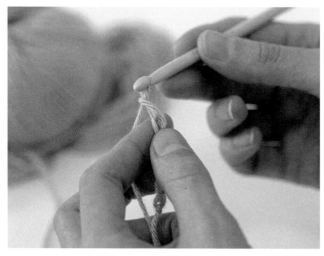

1 With the slip knot on your hook, take the yarn around the hook.

2 Gently pull the yarn through the loop on the hook, without tightening it too much.

Slip stitch

This stitch is mainly used either to join two pieces of crochet that have been made separately or to close a chain into a ring.

Making a slip stitch

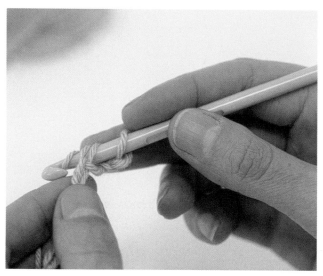

Insert the hook into the first chain stitch, picking up the two strands. Manipulate the hook under the yarn and then over it and catch it in the hook. Pull the yarn through both strands of the stitch and the loop on the hook.

Chain ring

A chain ring forms the basis for crochet worked in rounds. It is a short length of chain joined into a ring with a slip stitch.

Making a chain ring

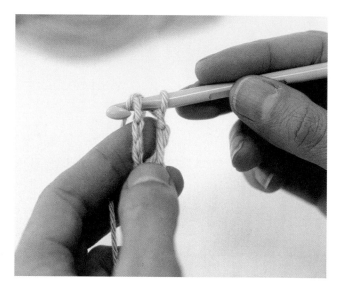

Insert the hook into the first chain stitch, picking up the two strands. Manipulate the hook under the yarn and then over it and catch it in the hook. Pull the yarn through both strands of the stitch and the loop on the hook.

Chain, chain, chains...

As you work, always insert the hook into the stitch from front to back—unless the pattern specifically instructs otherwise.

Insert the hook under the top two loops on the chain or stitch, unless the pattern specifically instructs otherwise.

When counting chains, do not count the loop on the hook, as it is there at both the beginning and end of each stitch.

Working a
Gauge Swatch

If you do not achieve the gauge stated, your project will not come out to the right measurements. Even the smallest difference in gauge can make a huge impact on your project, so it is important that you check your gauge before you start working.

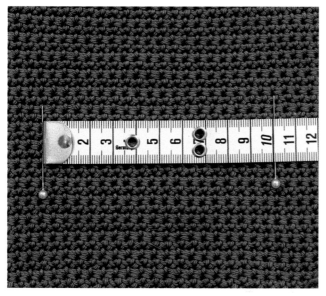

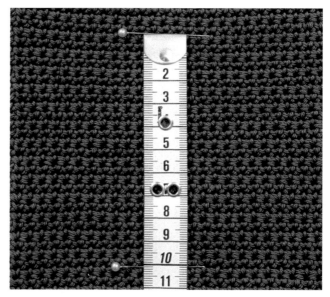

The gauge is usually measured across a 4 in. (10 cm) square, so using the yarn and hook size given for the gauge in the pattern, and using the same stitch, work a square of fabric that is slightly larger than this. Press the swatch and lay it flat, without stretching. Lay a tape or a metal ruler across horizontally and mark off 4 in. (10 cm) with two pins. Count the number of stitches between the pins. This is your stitch gauge.

Lay the ruler vertically and mark off 4 in. (10 cm) with two pins. Count the number of rows between the pins. Note that in the single crochet sample shown here, two rows of single crochet form one ridge so bear this in mind when counting rows. If you have more stitches and rows than given for the pattern gauge, try again with a size larger hook. If you have fewer stitches and rows than given for the pattern gauge, try again with a size smaller hook.

Making Fabrics

To make a flat fabric in crochet, use one or a
combination of the stitches detailed in this chapter
and work backwards and forwards in rows. Motifs in
crochet can also be worked from the center outward, which
is always referred to as working in rounds, although the
motifs themselves may be square.

Stitches

Learn these steps one at a time, and only progress to the next stitch
after you've fully mastered the one before.

Single crochet

This is a short stitch that makes quite a dense fabric. It is also sometimes used to join motifs, or to join two pieces of crochet together.

Making a single crochet stitch

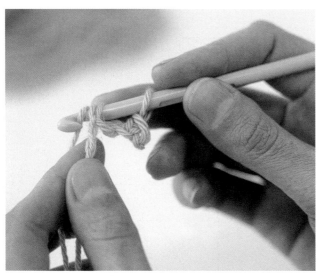

1 Insert the hook into the second chain from the hook, yarn over hook, then draw the yarn through the second chain only so you have two loops on the hook. Yarn over hook.

2 Draw the yarn through both loops on the hook. The abbreviation for this stitch in a pattern is "sc."

Half double crochet

This is a slightly taller stitch than single crochet, in which you loop the yarn over the hook first.

Making a half double crochet stitch

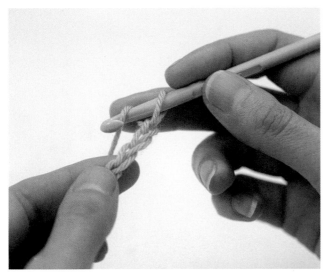

1 Yarn over hook, then insert the hook into the third chain from the hook.

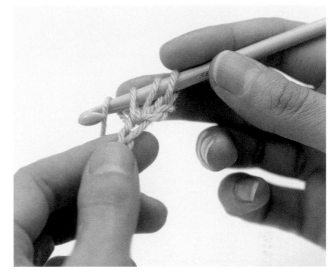

2 Yarn over hook, then draw the yarn through the third chain only so you have three loops on the hook, yarn over the hook again.

3 Draw the yarn through all three loops on the hook. The abbreviation for this stitch in a pattern is "hdc."

Double crochet

This is a taller stitch again, twice the height of single crochet, and very versatile.

Making a double crochet stitch

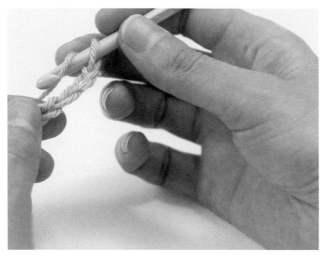

1 Yarn over hook, then insert the hook into the fourth chain from the hook.

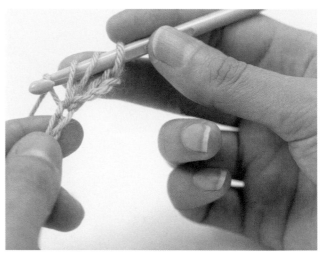

2 Yarn over hook, then draw the yarn through the fourth chain only so you have three loops on the hook, yarn over the hook again.

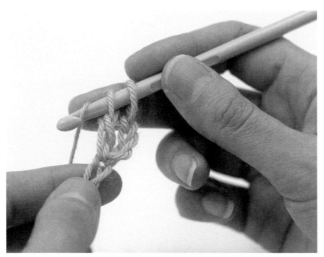

3 Draw the yarn through the first two loops on the hook.

4 Yarn over hook, then draw the yarn through the last two loops on the hook. The abbreviation for this stitch in a pattern is "dc."

Treble

This is a very high stitch, which will make quite an open fabric.

Making a treble crochet stitch

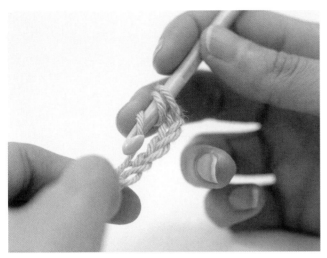

1 Yarn over hook twice, then insert the hook into the fifth chain from the hook.

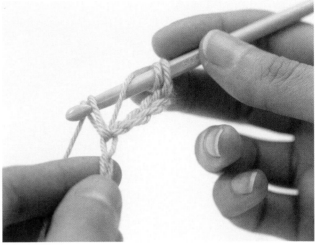

2 Yarn over hook, then draw the yarn through the fifth chain only, yarn over the hook again.

3 Draw the yarn through the first two loops on the hook only, yarn over hook again.

4 Draw the yarn through the next two loops on the hook and yarn over hook again, then draw through the last two loops on the hook. The abbreviation for this stitch in a pattern is "tr" or "trc."

Solomon's Knot

A Solomon's Knot is a lengthened chain stitch locked with a single crochet stitch worked into its back loop. Each knot is begun by lengthening the loop left on the hook to the required size.

Working Solomon's Knot

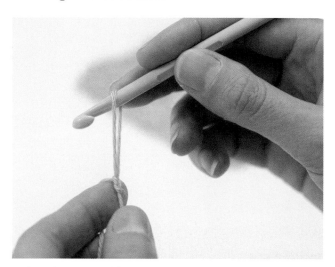

1 Chain 1 and lengthen the loop as required.

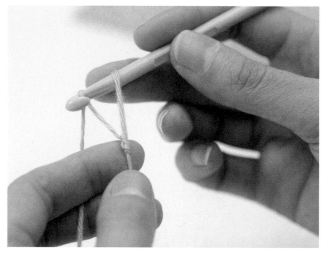

2 Wrap the yarn over the hook.

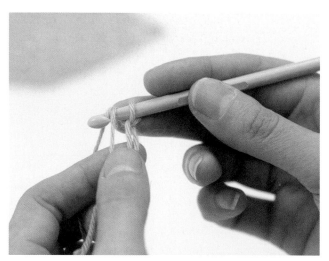

3 Draw through the loop on the hook, keeping the single back thread of this long chain separate from the 2 front threads.

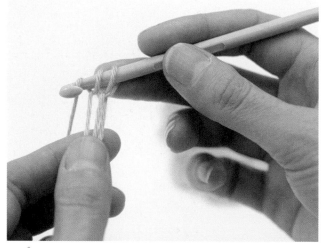

4 Insert the hook under this single back thread and wrap the yarn over the hook again.

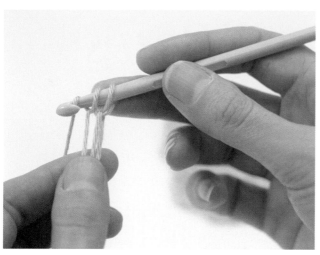

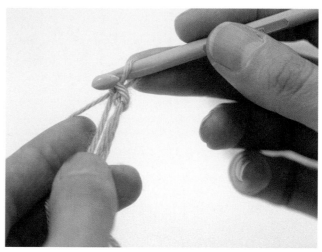

5 Draw a loop through and wrap the yarn over again.

6 Draw through both loops on the hook to complete the knot.

7 To begin a new row, miss the knot on the hook and the next 2 knots, and work a knot into the center of the third knot as shown and into every alternate knot thereafter. The loops on the second and subsequent rows should be about half again as long as those on the base row.

Rounds and Rows

When working in rounds, you do not usually turn the work, and the side facing you as you work is the right side of the fabric. Instead of a turning chain at the end of the row, you make a starting chain at the end of the round, again so the stitch can reach its proper height. With rows, you do turn the work.

Making rounds

1 Make three or more chains (the exact number depends on the design) and join them into a ring with a slip stitch.

2 To begin each round, make a starting chain to match the height of the stitches of the round. Always insert the hook into the center of the foundation chain ring to work the stitches of the first round.

3 On second and subsequent rows, after working the starting chain, insert the hook under the top two loops of the stitches in the previous round, unless otherwise instructed.

4 When each round is complete, insert the hook into the top of the starting chain and make a slip stitch to join the round.

Rows

To work in rows, first start by making a foundation chain with chain stitch (see page 22). After making your first stitch in single, half double, double, or treble, you just continue along the chain using your chosen stitch. At the beginning of the row, the first few chains in the foundation chain that have been missed allow the first stitch to stand up to its proper height. Together they look like and may be counted as the first stitch in the row. The number of chains missed therefore depends on the height of the stitch they are to match: single crochet = 1 chain missed; half double crochet = 2 chains missed; double crochet = 3 chains missed; treble crochet = four chains missed, and so on. The pattern will therefore tell you to make more chain stitches in your foundation chain than are required in the first row.

Making rows

1 Here the row is being worked in double crochet, so the 3 chains missed at the beginning are forming the first of eight stitches.

2 At the end of the row, turn the work to begin working back again. First work a turning chain—again the number of chains in the turning chain will depend on the stitch being used: single crochet = 1 chain; half double crochet = 2 chains; double crochet = 3 chains; treble crochet = four chains, and so on. Here three chains have been made for double crochet stitch. Again, these chain are often counted as the first stitch in the row.

3 At the end of the row, the last stitch is worked into the first stitch of the previous row—which will be the top of the turning chain of the previous row if this is being counted as the first stitch. If the turning chain is not being counted as the first stitch, miss it and work into the first proper stitch of the previous row instead. The pattern will state if the turning chain is being counted as a stitch or not.

Fastening off

Unlike knitting, when you finish a piece of crochet you should only have one stitch left on the hook so you do not have to bind off a row of stitches. If you have more than one loop on the hook at the finish, you have not completed the stitch correctly.

Fastening off the last stitch

Break the yarn and use the hook to pull the end through the loop, then tighten it.

Joining yarn

As you work, you may need to join in a new yarn, either because the ball has run out or because the pattern has involved fastening off in one piece and starting again on another—or perhaps for adding an edging.

Joining a new yarn on a new piece or for an edging

Insert the hook into the appropriate place, loop the yarn over, draw through and make 1 chain—or make the first loop with a slip knot as though starting a foundation chain.

Gripping yarns...

You can use the end of the yarn to join two pieces of work together, but you will need to leave a longer end so you have enough yarn to do this.

If you are planning to add an edging, it is best to join in a new ball of yarn as described right—even if the edging is in the same color as the crochet piece. It can be irritating if the yarn runs out halfway around your edging.

Some slippery yarns may be hard to fasten off as the last loop does not grip the end of the yarn properly even when you have pulled it tight, so try making a small knot instead.

Joining a new ball of yarn

1 Lay the new yarn across the tops of the stitches ahead and work over it—a contrasting color yarn is being used here only so it stands out.

2 After the change, work over the end of the old yarn for a few stitches. Trim both ends close to the fabric.

Changing color

1 When you are working whole rows in different colors, make the change in the last stitch in the row. Work the last stitch only up to the next to last step, so that two loops remain on the hook. Then pick up the new color and use this to complete the stitch.

2 Work the next stitch in the new color. Note that the top of this stitch will be in the new color, whereas if the previous stitch had been completed in the old color, that color would have encroached on the area of new color.

Shaping

*Shaping a piece of crochet is done by increasing and decreasing the number
of stitches in a row. This can be done either at the beginning or at the end of the row,
and the principle is the same whichever stitch you are working in. The steps below show
increasing done in double crochet and decreasing in single crochet.*

Increase at the beginning of a row

The new stitch is made by working into the stitch immediately next to the turning chain.

Increase at the end of a row

To increase at the end of a row, make two stitches into the same chain, as indicated.

Decreasing one stitch

1 To decrease one stitch in single crochet insert the hook in the next stitch, yarn over hook, draw through the work.

2 Insert the hook into the next stitch, yarn over, draw through the work, yarn over.

3 Draw through all three loops.

4 This leaves just one loop, so two stitches have become one. In the pattern this is abbreviated as "sc2tog."

Decreasing two stitches

Decreasing by two stitches (sc3tog) is done in the same way, except when you have three loops on the hook you insert the hook into the next stitch, yarn over, draw through the work, yarn over hook and draw through all four loops.

Decorative Techniques

Once you have mastered the basics of crochet,
it's easy to add interest with texture, using a variety of
techniques. Bobbles, which are known as popcorns, are
produced by working several times into the same stitch;
loop stitches can look like "fur;" and beads can be
incorporated as you work. Filet crochet is a delicate form
of crochet that can look like lace and is usually worked
with fine thread and a needle.

Popcorns

A popcorn is a group of complete stitches, usually worked into the same place,
folded and closed at the top. The number and type of stitches used varies.

Making a popcorn with 4 double crochet stitches

1 Work 4 double crochet in the normal way but into just one stitch; then take the hook out of the working loop.

2 Insert it under the top 2 loops of the first double in the group just made.

3 Pick up the working loop again. Draw this through to close up the group of stitches. The completed popcorn will project to the front.

Pop Art
If you make the popcorn on a background fabric of single crochet, it stands out more than against a double crochet fabric.

Popcorns are quite solid so they will retain their shape even after ironing.

If you want your popcorn to be more pronounced, you can work 6 doubles into the first stitch.

Loop Stitch

*Loop stitch is a variation of single crochet and is usually worked
on wrong side rows because the loops form at the back of the fabric.*

Working loop stitch

1 Insert the hook into the stitch below as usual.
Using a finger of the free hand, pull up the yarn
to form a loop of the required size. Pick up both
strands of the loop and draw them through.

2 Wrap the supply yarn over the hook.

Going Loopy!
The loop of yarn you make with your finger
determines the length of the final loops in the
fabric. If you plan to leave the loops as they are,
you need to try to keep the length of your loops
consistent as you work. If you want to cut them
to make a "fur" fabric, this is not quite so
important, as you can trim the ends so they all
match in length if necessary.

3 Draw the yarn through all 3 loops. You can cut
the loops afterward if you choose, to create
"fur," or leave them as loops.

Crochet with Beads

Introducing beads to a piece of crochet is a great way to add color and texture at the same time. Usually the beads are spaced out over the fabric, either in a random way or to create a pattern on the surface.

All the beads that you need should be added to the ball of yarn before you begin, as after you start working you can only add more beads by unraveling the whole ball and adding them from the other end—or by cutting the yarn. For this reason, it is a good idea to add a few more beads than you think you will need.

Working single crochet with beaded yarn

On a right side row, work to where the bead is to be placed. Insert the hook into the next stitch, move the bead up the yarn so it is close to the fabric, yarn over hook, draw through a loop, yarn over needle, draw through two loops on one hook.

Bead the Way

When choosing your beads, make sure they have a large enough hole to take the yarn you are using, but not so large that they will slide around too much as you work.

Match the size of the beads to the thickness of the yarn for a more subtle effect.

Beads that tone with the yarn add sparkle and texture. Contrasting beads give a more dramatic effect as they will stand out against the fabric.

Threading beads onto the yarn

The quickest way to thread beads onto the yarn is to use a needle and sewing thread. Thread the needle with a loop of sewing thread, then thread the end of the yarn through the loop. Thread the beads onto the needle and down onto the yarn.

Filet Crochet

Filet crochet is based on a simple network with a regular square grid, made of double and chain stitches.

The pattern instructions are usually presented in the form of squared charts, either with vertical lines representing double crochet stitches and horizontal lines chain stitches, or as a grid with a filled in square representing 3 doubles and a clear one representing two chains and a double.

Designs of all kinds—flowers, geometric patterns, lettering, and even pictorial scenes—are created by filling in some of the squares, or spaces, with double crochet stitches. Filet charts are read from the bottom to the top, right side rows from right to left and wrong side rows from left to right. Every row starts with three chain (count as one double), bringing the work to the correct height and balancing the pattern.

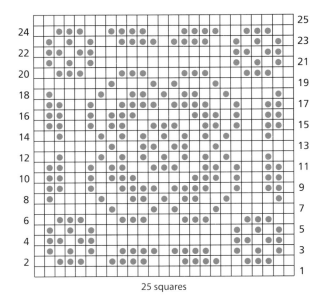

25 squares

Double Take

The most important thing with filet crochet is that the work is regular, with the lines all crossing at right angles.

You can easily draw up your own designs using a piece of graph paper. Filled in blocks will be the double crochet stitches, blank ones the chain stitches.

Filet crochet works best with fine, smooth yarns as the spaces need to be well defined for best results.

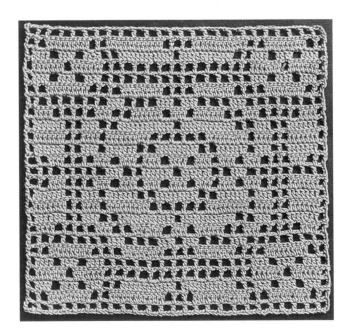

Finishing

After having spent some time making your project, you will want it to look its best. Before sewing pieces together, block and iron them carefully and choose the right stitch for the seam.

Blocking

This is the careful pinning of separate pieces of crochet before ironing to ensure they are the correct shape and measurements. This should always be done before joining seams. Blocking is very useful for smoothing out multicolor work, which often looks uneven, and for adjusting slightly the size or shape of a garment without re-making it.

For blocking and ironing you will need a flat, padded surface covered with a clean cloth—an ironing board with a thick towel fastened over it will do. A more professional blocking board is easy to make—just cover a large piece of wood with a layer of old towels or quilt batting, then cover in cotton gingham fabric, taking it around to the back and stapling into place. The geometric lines of the gingham will help you get edges straight. You will also need long dressmaker's pins with large colored heads, an iron and an ironing cloth.

To block an item, arrange the pieces of crochet wrong-side up on the padded surface. Place pins at intervals of around 1 in. (2.5 cm), angling them through the edge of the work into the padding, avoiding ribbed sections. Check that the measurements are correct and that the lines of stitches are straight in both horizontal and vertical directions. Re-pin if necessary to achieve the correct size and shape, stretching or easing slightly if required so that the outline forms a smooth edge between the pins.

Ironing and Damp Finishing

Each pinned-out section of crochet is ironed or damp-finished to give a smooth finish and help it to hold its shape. The characteristics of yarns vary greatly, and information on individual yarns is usually given on the ball band. If in doubt about ironing, always try ironing the gauge swatch first to avoid spoiling the actual garment. For wool, cotton, linen, and other natural yarns, use a damp cloth, steam thoroughly, but avoid letting the iron rest on the work.

Some types of crochet or parts of a garment are best left unironed, even if the yarn is suitable for ironing. These include bobbles and texture patterns as ironing may flatten the texture and blur the details. Damp finishing is more suitable in these cases. It is also suitable for fluffy and synthetic yarns—do not iron yarns that are 100% synthetic. For yarns that are a mixture (containing some natural fibers), use a cool iron over a dry cloth.

To iron, cover the pinned-out pieces with a damp or dry cloth, depending on the yarn. Check that the iron is the correct heat, then iron evenly and lightly, lifting the iron up and down to avoid dragging the crocheted material underneath. After ironing, remove a few pins. If the edge stays flat, take out all the pins and leave the piece to dry before removing it from the flat surface. If the edge curls when a few pins are removed, re-pin it and leave to dry with the pins in position. After joining the completed pieces of crochet, iron the seams lightly on the wrong side, using the same method as before but without pinning.

To damp finish, lay pieces on a damp (colorfast) towel, then roll them up together and leave for about an hour to allow the crochet to absorb the moisture from the towel. Unwrap, lay the damp towel on a flat surface and place the pieces on top of it. Ease the pieces into shape and pin as explained in Blocking, see opposite page. Lay another damp towel over the top, pat all over firmly to establish contact, then leave to dry.

Heatwave!

Always check the information on the ball band before ironing—some yarns may not be able to withstand the heat.

Never try to iron heavily textured patterns or bobbles as this will blur the details—you may be able to damp finish them instead, but if in doubt, leave well enough alone.

Fluffy yarns, such as mohair, can be brushed with a fine brush to finish them—particularly after the item has been washed.

Finishing

*Unlike knitting, in which the various pieces must be sewn together when they are finished,
most crochet patterns are designed so that the item is made in one piece. If you do have to
join pieces together the best way to do it is to crochet them together, using single crochet.*

On larger items, which are likely to drop over time, crocheted seams should stretch at the same rate as the rest
of the fabric—unlike sewn ones. If odd-shaped motifs need to be joined, the larger spaces between them can be
filled with smaller motifs of your choice. If sewing does seem to be the best option, it is best to use whipstitch.
Badly made joins can ruin a lovely piece of crochet, so it is worth spending a bit of time to get it right.

Joining with single crochet

Hold the two pieces of crochet with right sides
together. Insert the hook under one inside strand
only of the last stitch of each edge. Take the yarn
over the hook and pull through a loop, yarn over
again and pull through both loops. Continue
working in this way.

Whipstitch

Place the pieces wrong side up and with edges
together. Join with whipstitch as illustrated, using a
yarn needle and matching yarn.

Correcting Mistakes

It is far more difficult to correct mistakes in crochet than it is in knitting, because there is only one stitch on the hook most of the time. Since you cannot unravel just part of your work so easily, you have to unravel everything back to the error.

Look at the mistake carefully—does it really look wrong, or is it just a variation that may look deliberate? If the yarn is textured or fluffy, the odd incorrect stitch may not show very much. The best way to handle a major problem that you really cannot live with is to unravel and begin again. It sounds rather drastic, but at least you will be learning and hopefully you will not make the same mistake again. You may be able to add a motif or some surface crochet to hide small mistakes, but do try to look at the item as a whole to be sure that they will not ruin the look of the piece in themselves.

Problem Solving

Check what you are doing at regular intervals so any problem is quickly spotted before you have gone too much further.

Large, heavy pieces of crochet may drop after they have been worn or hung up for some time. Blocking and ironing can help to get them back into shape.

To prevent items dropping in the first place, while you are making the piece try pinning your work to a padded hanger and letting it hang between times when you are not working on it.

Fashion

Whether you want to create a Boho-Chic Shrug or a vibrant Ruffled Mohair Cardigan, the mixture of exciting and classic styles in this chapter will keep you looking your best from day to night.

Ruffled Mohair Cardigan

Look feminine and pretty in Sophie Britten's gorgeous tie-front cardigan,
accented with sumptuous ruffles around the edges. The mohair yarn hides the detail
of the stitches and the cardigan is worked in simple single crochet.

Materials

Yarn
Mohair by Colinette, 3½oz/100g hank, each
   approx 190 yd/175 m
   (78% mohair, 13% wool, 9% nylon)
5 (6, 7) hanks in Cherry

Hooks and extras
M/13 (9.00 mm) crochet hook

Gauge
9 sc and 10 rows to 4 in. (10 cm) over single
   crochet fabric using an M/13 (9.00 mm) hook.
   Change hook size, if necessary, to obtain this
   gauge.

Sizes and Measurements
To fit: bust 32–34 (34–38, 38–40) in. [81–86
(86–97, 97–102) cm]
Actual measurements: width 15¾ (17¼, 19¼) in.
[40 (44, 49) cm]; **length** 19 (20½, 22) in. [48 (52,
56) cm]; **sleeve** 19½ (20, 20½) in. [50 (51, 52) cm]

Back
Ch 37 (41, 45).
Row 1 (WS): 1 sc into 2nd ch from hook, 1sc into
each ch to end, turn: 36 (40, 44) sc.
Row 2: 1 ch, 1 sc into each sc to end, turn.
Work a further 27 (29, 31) rows in sc..

Shape armholes:
Next row: Ss across 2 sc, 1 ch, sc2tog, 1 sc into
each sc to last 4 sc, sc2tog, turn: 30 (34, 38) sts.
Next row: 1 ch, sc2tog over next 2 sc, 1 sc into each
sc to last 2 sts, sc2tog: 28 (32, 36) sts.
Rep last row once: 26 (30, 34) sts.
Continue straight until armholes measure 6¾ (7½,
8½) in. [17 (19, 21) cm].
Fasten off.

Left Front

Ch 31 (35, 39).

Row 1: 1 sc into 2nd ch from hook, 1 sc into each ch to end, turn: 30 (34, 38) sc.

Row 2 (RS): 1 ch, 1 sc into each sc to last 2 sc, sc2tog, turn.

Row 3: 1 ch, 1sc into each sc, turn.

Rep rows 2 and 3 until 16 (19, 22) sts rem, ending at unshaped edge.

Shape armholes:

Next row: Ss across first 2 sc, 1 ch, sc2tog, 1sc into each sc to last 2 sts, sc2tog, turn: 12 (15, 18) sts.

Next row: 1 ch, 1sc into each sc to last 2 sts, sc2tog, turn: 11 (14, 17) sts.

Next row: 1 ch, sc2tog, 1 sc in each sc to last 2 sc, sc2tog, turn: 9 (12, 15) sts.

Cont straight until armhole measures 6¾ (7½, 8½) in. [17 (19, 21) cm].

Fasten off.

Right Front

Work to match Left Front, reversing shapings.

Sleeves

Ch 21 (23, 25).

Row 1: 1 sc into 2nd ch from hook, 1 sc into each ch to end, turn: 20 (22, 24) sc.

Inc 1 st at each end of 9th and every following 6th row until there are 26 (28, 30) sts.

Cont straight until sleeve measures 23½ (24, 24½) in. [60 (61, 62) cm].

Shape top of sleeve:

Next row: Ss across first 3 sc, 1 sc into each sc to last 3 sc, turn.

Next row: 1 ch, sc2tog, 1 sc into each sc to last 2 sc, sc2tog, turn: 18 (20, 22) sts.

Rep the last row 6 (7, 8) times: 6 sts.

Fasten off.

Finishing

Join 6 (7, 8) sts at each end for shoulder seams. Match center top of each sleeve to shoulder seam, set in sleeves. Join side seams. Join sleeve seams leaving a vent opening of 4 in. (10 cm) at the cuff.

Make body ruffles:

With RS facing and M/13 (9.00 mm) hook, attach yarn to center back of neck.

Round 1: 2 sc into each sc and row end across back neck, down Left Front, along lower edge of Left Front, Back, Right Front and then up Right Front and across back neck, ss into first sc.

Round 2: 2 sc into each sc to end, ss into first sc. Fasten off.

Make collar:

Row 1: With RS facing rejoin yarn to top corner of Right Front, 1 sc into each sc to top corner of Left Front, turn.

Row 2: 3 ch, 1 dc into each sc of row 1. Fasten off.

Make sleeve ruffles:

With RS facing and M/13 (9.00 mm) hook, attach yarn to top of sleeve vent.

Row 1: 2 sc into each sc and row end along one side of vent, around the cuff and up the other side of the vent, ss into first sc, turn.

Row 2: 1 ch, 2 sc into each st to end, ss into first sc. Fasten off.

Tank Top

Designed by Sue Whiting, this classic tank top is worked in a striking hand-dyed, pure silk yarn. Simple to make, the clever shell effect pattern combines just doubles, chains, and single crochet.

Materials

Yarn
Tao by Colinette, 1¾oz/50g hank, each approx 128 yd/117 m (100% pure silk)
6 (6, 6, 7, 7, 7) hanks in Florentina 48

Hooks and extras
3.00 mm crochet hook
E/4 (3.50 mm) crochet hook

Gauge
24 sts and 12 rows to 4 in. (10cm) measured over pattern using E/4 (3.50 mm) hook. Change hook size, if necessary, to obtain this gauge.

Sizes and Measurements
To fit: bust 32 (34, 36, 38, 40, 42) in. [81 (86, 91, 97, 102, 107) cm]

Actual measurements: width 34 (36, 38, 40, 42, 43¼) in. [86 (91, 96, 101, 106, 110) cm]; **length** 19 (19¼, 19½, 20, 20½, 20¾) in. [48 (49, 50, 51, 52, 53) cm]

Back and Front
With E/4 (3.50 mm) hook, ch 104 (110, 116, 122, 128, 134).

Foundation row (RS): 1 sc into 2nd ch from hook, *skip 2 ch, [1 dc, 1 ch, 1 dc, 1 ch and 1 dc] into next ch, skip 2 ch, 1 sc into next ch; rep from * to end, turn: 17 (18, 19, 20, 21, 22) patt reps.

Now cont in patt

Row 1 (WS): 4 ch (counts as first dc and 1 ch), 1 dc into sc at base of 4 ch, *skip [1 dc and 1 ch], 1 sc into next dc, skip [1 ch and 1 dc]**, [1 dc, 1 ch, 1 dc, 1 ch and 1 dc] into next sc; rep from * to end, ending last rep at **, [1 dc, 1 ch and 1 dc] into last sc, turn.

Row 2: 1 ch (does NOT count as st), 1 sc into dc at end of previous row, *skip [1 ch and 1 dc], [1 dc, 1 ch, 1 dc, 1 ch and 1 dc] into next sc, skip [1 dc and 1 ch], 1 sc into next dc; rep from * to end, working sc at end of last rep into 3rd of 4 ch at beg of previous row, turn.

Rows 1 and 2 form patt.

Cont in patt until work measures approx 11 (11½, 11½, 11¾, 11¾, 12¼) in. [28 (29, 29, 30, 30, 31) cm], ending after a row 2 and a RS row.

Shape armholes
Next row (WS): Ss across 1 sc, 1 dc, 1 ch and into next dc, 1 ch (does NOT count as st), 1 sc into same place as last ss – ½ patt rep decreased, *skip [1 ch and 1 dc], [1 dc, 1 ch, 1 dc, 1 ch and 1 dc] into next sc, skip [1 dc and 1 ch], 1 sc into next dc; rep from * until [1 ch, 1 dc and 1 sc] rem at end of row and turn, leaving rem 3 sts unworked—½ patt rep

decreased: 16 (17, 18, 19, 20, 21) patt reps.
Rep last row 6 (7, 7, 8, 8, 9) times more: 10 (10, 11, 11, 12, 12) patt reps.
Work 1 row, ending after a row 1.

Shape neck
Next row: 1 ch (does NOT count as st), 1 sc into dc at end of previous row, *skip [1 ch and 1 dc], [1 dc, 1 ch, 1 dc, 1 ch and 1 dc] into next sc, skip [1 dc and 1 ch], 1 sc into next dc; rep from * 2 (2, 2, 2, 3, 3) times more and turn, leaving rem 7 (7, 8, 8, 8, 8) patt reps unworked.
Cont on these 3 (3, 3, 3, 4, 4) patt reps only for first side of neck.

Working all decreases in same way as for armhole, dec ½ patt rep at neck edge of next 2 rows: 2 (2, 2, 2, 3, 3) patt reps.

Cont straight until armhole measures 7½ (7½, 7¾, 7¾, 8¼, 8¼) in. [19 (19, 20, 20, 21, 21) cm], ending after a WS row.

Fasten off.

Return to last complete row worked, skip center 3 (3, 4, 4, 3, 3) patt reps, rejoin yarn to dc at center of next [1 dc, 1 ch, 1 dc, 1 ch and 1 dc] group, 1 ch (does NOT count as st), 1 sc into same dc as where yarn was rejoined, patt to end, turn: 3 (3, 3, 3, 4, 4) patt reps.

Complete second side to match first, reversing shaping.

Finishing

Join side and shoulder seams.

Make neck edging

With RS facing and using 3.00 mm hook, attach yarn at one shoulder seam and work around neck edge as follows: 1 ch (does NOT count as st), work 1 round of sc evenly around entire neck edge, ending with ss to first sc, turn.

Next round: 1 ch (does NOT count as st), 1 sc into each sc to end, ss to first sc, turn.

Rep last round twice more, working sc2tog as required to ensure edging lays flat.

Fasten off.

Make armhole edgings

Work as given for neck edging, rejoining yarn at top of side seam.

Make hem edging

Work as given for neck edging, rejoining yarn at base of one side seam.

Think Tank

The pure silk yarn gives this top a really luxurious feel, but be sure to follow the special care instructions to be found on the ball band when it needs cleaning.

For a slightly different look, you could make the neck and armhole edging in a contrasting color, or choose a plain color to match one of the shades in the multicolor yarn.

If you need your top a little bit longer than the dimensions given, you can work a few more rows before beginning the shaping for the armholes.

Fringed Poncho

A warm and woolly poncho adds color and zing to a spring day. This piece is very simple to make as it is worked in rounds and made in just one piece. Designed by Sophie Britten, the garment is finished with a long fringe of tassels.

Materials

Yarn

Big Wool by Rowan, 3½oz/100g ball, each approx
     88 yd/80 m (100% wool)

5 (5, 6) balls of Smooch (A)

1 ball of Whoosh (B)

Hooks and extras

K/10½ (6.50 mm) hook

M/13 (9.00 mm) hook (for tassels)

Gauge

7½ sts and 3 rows to 4 in. (10 cm) measured over
     doubles using K10½ (6.50 mm) hook. Change
     hook size, if necessary, to obtain this gauge.

Special abbreviations

Shell = work [2 dc, 2 ch, 2 dc] into next st.

Sizes and Measurements

To fit: bust 30–32 (34–36, 38–40) in. [76–81 (86–97, 97–102) cm]

Actual measurements: length at center front 21 (22, 24) in. [53 (56, 61) cm]

Front

Using A and K10½ (6.50 mm) crochet hook, ch 60 (64, 68) for neck edge, join with a ss to first ch, making sure you don't twist the base ch.

Round 1: 3 ch, 1 dc into each ch to end: 60 (64, 68) sts.

Round 2: 3 ch (count as 1 dc), [1 dc into each of next 14 (15, 16) sts, 2 dc into next st] three times, 1 dc into each of next 14 (15, 16) sts, 1 dc into st at base of 3 ch, ss into top of 3 ch: 64 (68, 72) sts.

Round 3: 3 ch, [1 dc into each of next 15 (16, 17) sts, 2 dc into next st] three times, 1 dc into each of next 15 (16, 17) sts, 1 dc into st at base of 3 ch, ss into top of 3 ch: 68 (72, 76) sts.

Round 4: 3 ch, [1 dc into each of next 16 (17, 18) sts, 2 dc into next st] three times, 1 dc into each of next 16 (17, 18) sts, 1 dc into st at base of 3 ch, ss into top of 3 ch: 72 (74, 80) sts.

Round 5: 3 ch, [1 dc into each of next 17 (18, 19) sts, 2 dc into next st] three times, 1 dc into each of next 17 (18, 19) sts, 1 dc into st at base of 3 ch, ss into top of 3 ch: 76 (80, 84) sts.

Round 6: 3 ch, [1 dc into each of next 18 (19, 20) sts, 2 dc into next st] three times, 1 dc into each of next 18 (19, 20) sts, 1 dc into st at base of 3 ch, ss into top of 3 ch: 80 (84, 88) sts.

Round 7: 3 ch, [1 dc into each of next 19 (20, 21) sts, 2 dc into next st] three times, 1 dc into each of next 19 (20, 21) sts, 1 dc into st at base of 3 ch, ss into top of 3 ch: 84 (88, 92) sts.

Round 8: 3 ch, [1 dc into each of next 20 (21, 22) sts, 2 dc into next st] three times, 1 dc into each of next 20 (21, 22) sts, 1 dc into st at base of 3 ch, ss into top of 3 ch: 88 (92, 96) sts.

Round 9: 3 ch, 1 dc into each of next 21 (22, 23) sts, 2 dc into next st, 1 dc into each of next 43 (45, 47) sts, 2 dc into next st, 1 dc into each of next 21 (22, 23) sts, ss into top of 3 ch: 90 (94, 98) sts.

Round 10: 3 ch (count as 1 dc), 1 dc into each of next 21 (22, 23) dc, skip 1 dc, work 1 shell into next dc, skip 1 dc, 1 dc into each of next 42 (44, 46) dc, skip 1 dc, 1 shell into next dc, miss 1 dc, 1 dc into each of next 20 (21, 22) dc, ss into top of 3 ch.

Round 11: 3 ch (count as 1 dc), [1 dc into each dc to shell, 1 dc into first dc of shell, skip next dc of shell, 1 shell into 2 ch sp at center of shell, skip last 2 dc of shell] twice, 1 dc into each dc, ss to top of 3 ch.
Rep round 11 until poncho measures 21 (22, 24) in. [53 (56, 61) cm] at center point.
Fasten off.

Tassels

Using a piece of card 7 in. (18 cm) wide, wrap B around card, cut along one edge of the card to give strands 14 in. (36 cm) long.
Divide the strands into bundles of 4 strands. Fold a bundle in half, draw the center of the bundle through a bottom edge stitch on the poncho using the M/13 (9.00 mm) crochet hook, feed the ends through the loop and pull tight. Place the tassels evenly all the way around the bottom edge of the poncho. Trim ends.

Poncho Panache

This poncho is made all in one piece so there is no sewing or joining of seams required at the end—as soon as you have finished making it, you can put it straight on!

The fringe here has been made in a toning color yarn, but you could either use the same yarn as used for the body of the poncho, or choose something much more contrasting for a brighter effect.

For a shorter poncho, perhaps with the sides finishing at elbow length instead of at the wrist, just stop repeating row 11 around 4–6 in. (10–15 cm) before you reach the dimension given here for the center point.

Beaded fringe can look great—thread a suitable bead onto two or three strands of each bundle of fringe and knot beneath to keep the beads in place. Choose washable beads if you want to wash the poncho when it gets dirty—otherwise you will either have to dry clean it or remove the beads each time!

Boho-Chic Shrug

Simple square motifs are joined while they are worked to create this shrug designed by Sue Whiting. The edges are finished with neat single crochet borders.

Materials

Yarn
Summer Tweed by Rowan, 1¾oz/50g ball, each
   approx 117 yd/108 m (70% silk, 30% cotton)
8 balls in Blossom 541

Hooks and extras
G/6 (4.00 mm) crochet hook

Gauge
One motif measures 6 in. (15 cm) square using G/6
   (4.00 mm) hook. Change hook size, if necessary,
   to obtain this gauge.

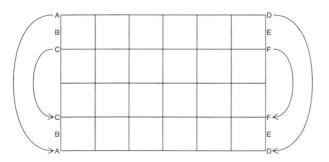

Sizes and Measurements
To fit: bust 32–40 in. (81–102 cm)
Actual measurements: width at opening edge
71 in. (180 cm); **length laid flat** 13¾ in. (35 cm)

Motif
Chain 6 and join with a ss to form a ring.
Round 1 (RS): 3 ch (counts as 1 dc), 15 dc into ring, ss to top of 3 ch at beg of round: 16 sts.
Round 2: 5 ch (counts as 1 dc and 2 ch), miss st at base of 5 ch, [1 dc into next dc, 2 ch] 15 times, ss to 3rd of 5 ch at beg of round: 16 ch sps.
Round 3: Ss into first ch sp, 3 ch (counts as first dc), 2 dc into same ch sp, *1 ch, miss 1 dc, 3 dc into next ch sp; rep from * to end, 1 sc into top of 3 ch at beg of round.
Round 4: Ss into ch sp formed by sc at end of last round, 1 ch (does NOT count as st), 1 sc into same ch sp, *[3 ch, miss 3 dc, 1 sc into next ch sp] twice, 6 ch, miss 3 dc, 1 sc into next ch sp, 3 ch, miss 3 dc, 1 sc into next ch sp; rep from * to end, replacing sc at end of last rep with ss to first sc.
Round 5: Ss into first ch sp, 3 ch (counts as first dc), 2 dc into same ch sp, *3 ch, ss to top of last dc worked, 3 dc into next ch sp, 3 ch, ss to top of last dc worked, (5 dc, 4 ch, ss to 3rd ch from hook, 1 ch and 5 dc) into next ch sp**, [3 ch, ss to top of last dc worked, 3 dc into next ch sp] twice; rep from * to end, ending last rep at **, 3 ch, ss to top of last dc worked, 3 dc into next ch sp, 3 ch, ss to top of last

dc worked, ss to top of 3 ch at beg of round. Fasten off.

Basic motif forms a square. In each corner there is a 3-ch loop between 2 blocks of 5 dc, and along each side there are a further four 3-ch loops. Join motifs while working round 5 by replacing each (3 ch) loop with (1 ch, ss into corresponding ch loop of adjacent motif, 1 ch).

Shrug

Following diagram, make and join 24 motifs to form one large rectangle 6 motifs wide and 4 motifs long. While joining motifs, also join "side seams" by joining side motifs as indicated on diagram—join A to A, B to B and so on. Completed joined section will form a "bag" shape, 6 motifs wide and 2 motifs deep. Openings left at "base corners" of "bag" form armhole openings.

Body Opening Edging

With RS facing, rejoin yarn with a ss into joined corner point indicated by A on diagram, 1 ch (does NOT count as st, 1 sc into joined corner point, now work around entire opening edge as follows: *4 ch, 1 sc into next ch loop, 3 ch, 1 sc into next ch loop, 2 ch, 1 sc into next ch loop, 3 ch, 1 sc into next ch loop, 4 ch, 1 sc into next joined corner point; rep from * to end, replacing sc at end of last rep with ss to first sc: 60 ch sps.

Next round (RS): 1 ch (does NOT count as st), 1 sc into first sc, *4 sc into next ch sp, 1 sc into sc, 3 sc into next ch sp, 1 sc into next sc, 2 sc into next ch sp, 1 sc into sc, 3 sc into next ch sp, 1 sc into next sc, 4 sc into next ch sp**, 1 sc into next sc; rep from * to end, ending last rep at **, ss to first sc, turn: 252 sts.

Next round: 1 ch (does NOT count as st), 1 sc into each sc to end, ss to first sc, turn.
Rep last round 4 times more.
Fasten off.

Armhole edgings

With RS facing, rejoin yarn with a ss into joined corner point indicated by C (or F) on diagram, 1 ch (does NOT count as st, 1 sc into joined corner point, now work around armhole opening edge as follows: *4 ch, 1 sc into next ch loop, 3 ch, 1 sc into next ch loop, 2 ch, 1 sc into next ch loop, 3 ch, 1 sc into next ch loop, 4 ch**, 1 sc into next joined corner point; rep from * to ** once more, ss to first sc: 10 ch sps.

Next round (RS): 1 ch (does NOT count as st), 1 sc into first sc, *4 sc into next ch sp, 1 sc into sc, 3 sc into next ch sp, 1 sc into next sc, 2 sc into next ch sp, 1 sc into sc, 3 sc into next ch sp, 1 sc into next sc, 4 sc into next ch sp**, 1 sc into next sc; rep from * to end, ending last rep at **, ss to first sc, turn: 42 sts.

Next round: 1 ch (does NOT count as st), 1 sc into each sc to end, ss to first sc, turn.
Rep last round twice more.
Fasten off.

Finishing

Block and iron garments following the instructions on the ball band.

Heirloom Capelet

*Sue Whiting's ultra-feminine capelet features a lacy
edging in a wispy kid mohair yarn and ties at the neck. Wear it
over a silk dress for a lovely night on the town.*

Materials

Yarn

4 ply Soft by Rowan, 1¾oz/50g ball, each approx
    190 yd/175 m (100% merino wool)
5 (6, 6) balls in Day Dream 378 (A)
2 (3, 3) balls in Dewberry 600 (B)

Hooks and extras

2.50 mm crochet hook
E/4 (3.50 mm) crochet hook

Gauge

19 sts and 14 rows to 4 in. (10 cm) measured over
    pattern using E/4 (3.50 mm) hook and A.
    Change hook size, if necessary, to obtain this
    gauge.

Special Abbreviations

hdc2tog = [yo and insert hook as indicated, yo
    and draw loop through] twice, yo and draw
    through all 5 loops on hook

Sizes and Measurements

To fit: bust 32–34 (36–38, 40–42) in. [81–86
(91–97, 102–107) cm]
Actual measurements: width at lower edge 63
(67, 71¼) in. [160 (171, 181) cm]; **length** 17¼ (18,
19) in. [44 (46, 48) cm]

Back

With E/4 (3.50 mm) hook and A, chain 154 (164,
174).
Row 1 (RS): 1 dc into 4th ch from hook, 1 dc into
each ch to end, turn: 152 (162, 172) sts.
Row 2: 2 ch (counts as first hdc), skip st at base of 2
ch, 1 hdc into each dc to end, working last hdc into
top of 3 ch at beg of previous row, turn.
Row 3: 1 ch (does NOT count as st), 1 sc into each
hdc to end, working last sc into top of 2 ch at beg of
previous row, turn.
Row 4: 3 ch (counts as first dc), skip st at base of 3
ch, 1 dc into each sc to end, turn.
Rows 5 and 6: As rows 2 and 3.
Row 7: 3 ch (counts as first dc), skip st at base of 3
ch, working into back loops only of sts of previous
row: 1 dc into each sc to end, turn.

Now cont in patt.
Rows 8 and 9: As rows 2 and 3.
Row 10: As row 4.
Rows 8 to 10 form patt.

Cont in patt, shaping sides as follows:

Row 11: 2 ch (does NOT count as st), skip st at base of 2 ch—1 st decreased, 1 hdc into each dc to last 2 sts, hdc2tog over next hdc and top of 3 ch at beg of previous row—1 st decreased, turn: 150 (160, 170) sts.

Work 5 rows.

Row 17: As row 11: 148 (158, 168) sts.

Work 3 rows.

Row 21: 1 ch (does NOT count as st), sc2tog over first 2 hdc—1 st decreased, 1 sc into each hdc to last 2 sts, sc2tog over next hdc and top of 2 ch at beg of previous row—1 st decreased, turn: 146 (156, 166) sts.

Work 1 row.

Row 23: As row 11: 144 (154, 164) sts.

Work 1 row.

Row 25: 3 ch (does NOT count as st), skip st at base of 3 ch—1 st decreased, 1 dc into each sc to last 2 sc, dc2tog over last 2 sc—1 st decreased, turn: 142 (152, 162) sts.

Working all decreases as now set, cont in patt, shaping side seams by dec 1 st at each end of 2nd (2nd, next) and foll 3 (1, 0) alt rows, then on foll 13 (20, 26) rows, ending after a row of dc: 108 sts.

Shape shoulders:

Next row: Ss across and into 3rd st, 2 ch (counts as first hdc)—2 sts decreased, 1 hdc into each dc to last 2 sts and turn, leaving last 2 sts unworked—2 sts decreased: 104 sts.

Next row: Ss across and into 3rd st, 1 ch (does NOT count as st), 1 sc into same place as last ss—2 sts decreased, 1 sc into each hdc to last 2 sts and turn, leaving last 2 sts unworked—2 sts decreased: 100 sts.

Next row: Ss across and into 4th st, 3 ch (counts as first dc)—3 sts decreased, 1 dc into each sc to last 3 sts and turn, leaving last 3 sts unworked—3 sts decreased: 94 sts.

Working all decreases as set by last 3 rows, dec 3 sts at each end of next row, 4 sts at each end of foll 2 rows, then 5 sts at each end of foll 4 rows, ending after a row of hdc: 32 sts.

Fasten off.

Left Front

With E/4 (3.50 mm) hook and A, chain 78 (83, 88).

Row 1 (RS): 1 dc into 4th ch from hook, 1 dc into each ch to end, turn: 76 (81, 86) sts.

Work rows 2 to 10 as given for Back.

Rows 8 to 10 form patt.

Working all shaping in same way as given for Back, cont in patt, shaping side seam by dec 1 st at beg of next and foll 6th row, then on foll 4th row, then on foll 6 (4, 2) alt rows, then at same edge on foll 13 (20, 27) rows, ending after a row of dc: 54 sts.

Shape shoulder and neck:

Working all shaping as set by Back, dec 2 sts at side seam shaped edge and 10 sts at front opening edge of next row: 42 sts.

Dec 1 st at neck edge of next 6 rows and at same time dec 2 sts at side seam edge of next row, 3 sts at side seam edge of foll 2 rows, 4 sts at side seam edge of foll 2 rows, then 5 sts at side seam edge of foll row: 15 sts.

Dec 5 sts at side seam edge of foll 2 rows, ending after a row of dc: 5 sts.

Fasten off.

Right Front

Work as given for Left Front, reversing all shaping.

Finishing

Join side and shoulder seams.

Lower Ruffle:

With RS facing, using 2.50 mm hook and B, attach yarn at base of Left Front opening edge and work along foundation edge as follows: 1 ch (does NOT count as st), 1 sc into foundation ch where yarn was attached, 2 sc into each of next 74 (79, 84) ch of Left Front, 1 sc into last ch of Left Front, 1 sc into first ch of Back, 2 sc into each of next 149 (159, 169) ch of Back, 1 sc into each of last 2 ch of Back, 1 sc into first ch of Right Front, 2 sc into each of next 74 (79, 84) ch of Right Front, 1 sc into last ch of Right Front, ending at base of Right Front opening edge, turn: 601 (641, 681) sts.

Row 2 (WS): 1 ch (does NOT count as st), 1 sc into each sc to end, turn.

Row 3: 1 ch (does NOT count as st), 1 sc into each of first 3 sc, *9 ch, skip 3 sc**, 1 sc into each of next 5 sc; rep from * to end, ending last rep at **, 1 sc into each of last 3 sc, turn: 75 (80, 85) patt repeats.

Row 4: 1 ch (does NOT count as st), 1 sc into each of first 2 sc, *5 ch, skip 1 sc, 1 sc into next ch sp, 5 ch, skip 1 sc**, 1 sc into each of next 3 sc; rep from * to end, ending last rep at **, 1 sc into each of last 2 sc, turn.

Row 5: 1 ch (does NOT count as st), 1 sc into first sc, *5 ch, skip [1 sc and 5 ch], 1 sc into next sc, 5 ch, skip [5 ch and 1 sc], 1 sc into next sc; rep from * to end, turn.

Row 6: 1 ch (does NOT count as st), 1 sc into first sc, *5 ch, skip 5 ch, [1 ss, 7 ch, 1 ss, 7 ch, 1 ss, 7 ch and 1 ss] into next sc, 5 ch, skip 5 ch, 1 sc into next sc; rep from * to end.
Fasten off.

Upper Ruffle:

Work as given for Lower Ruffle but working into front loops of row 6 of Fronts and Back, instead of foundation ch edge.

Front Edgings:

With RS facing, using E/4 (3.50 mm) hook and A, attach yarn and work 1 row of sc evenly along each front opening edge, leaving ends of ruffles free. Fasten off.

Neck Tie and Border

With E/4 (3.50 mm) hook and A, ch 60.
Fasten off and set this length of ch to one side.
With E/4 (3.50 mm) hook and A, ch 61, 1 sc into 2nd ch from hook, 1 sc into each ch to end, now with RS facing and starting at top of Right Front opening edge, work 1 row of sc evenly around entire neck edge, ending at top of Left Front opening edge, pick up length of ch set to one side and work 1 sc into each ch to end, turn.

Next row: 1 ch (does NOT count as st), 1 sc into each sc to end, turn.
Rep last row 4 times more.
Fasten off.

Lace Up

The double lacy ruffle around the bottom makes this pretty capelet look really feminine, but you could easily make just the lower ruffle and omit the upper one if you prefer something a little bit plainer.

The ruffle is made here in a yarn that tones with the main capelet, but two contrasting yarns would look equally pretty. Try a crisp blue and pure white for a fresh summery look, or black and bright red for a more dramatic effect.

Accessories

Crochet accessories make speedy projects and great little gifts for friends and family. The Granny-Square Scarf is an attractive way to use up some of that leftover yarn, while the Beaded Bag holds all those essential items for a fun evening out.

Filet Hairband

Sophie Britten's pretty hairband uses the classic technique of filet crochet to create an open mesh strip that ties with a single crochet chain. You can make it a bit longer if you wish, but the ties are adjustable to fit most head sizes. Filet crochet patterns are often illustrated with a chart, but the pattern here is simple.

Materials

Yarn
Cotton Glace by Rowan, 1¾oz/50g ball, each approx 125 yd/115 m (100% cotton)
1 ball in Zeal

Hooks and extras
US 6 (4.00 mm) crochet hook

Gauge
11 blocks and 10 rows to 4 in. (10 cm) measured over double filet, using US 6 (4.00 mm) hook. Change hook size, if necessary, to obtain this gauge.

Special abbreviations
Sc2tog = [insert hook into next st, yrh, draw through a loop] twice, yrh, draw through all 3 loops on hook—1 st decreased.

Sc3tog = [insert hook into next st, yrh, draw through a loop] three times, yrh, draw through all 4 loops on hook—2 sts decreased.

Sizes and Measurements
To fit: average-size head

Hairband
Ch 2.

Row 1: 3 sc into 2nd ch from hook, turn.

Row 2: 1 ch, 2 sc into first st, 1 sc into next st, 2 sc into last st, turn: 5 sts.

Cont in sc, inc by 1 st at each end of next 3 rows: 11 sts.

Next Row: 4 ch (count as 1 dc and 1 ch), skip 2 sts, 1 dc into next st, *1 ch, skip 1 st, 1 dc into next st; rep from * to end, turn.

Next Row: 4 ch (count as 1 dc and 1 ch) skip 2 sts, 1 dc into next st, *1 ch, skip 1 st, 1 dc into next st; rep from * to end, working last dc into 3rd ch of 4 ch, turn.

Rep last row until the hairband measures 14 in. (36 cm).

Next Row: Counting each ch as a st, sc2tog, 1 sc into each st to last 2 sts, sc2tog, turn: 9 sts.

Next Row: Sc2tog, 1 sc into each sc to last 2 sts, sc2tog, turn: 7 sts.

Rep last row twice: 3 sts.

Next Row: sc3tog.

Without turning, work 1 round of sc evenly around outside of headband, working 2 sc into each filet block, ss into first sc. Do not fasten off.

Tie

Make a single chain as follows: *insert hook under left loop of the stitch you have just made, yrh and draw through a loop, yrh, draw through 2 loops; rep from * until tie measures 12 in. (30 cm) long. Fasten off.

Rejoin yarn in center of other end of hairband, 1 sc into center st and work a single chain as before. Fasten off.

Granny-Square Scarf

*These familiar motifs are timeless and quick to work, and the strips of motifs
at both ends of this scarf make a novel variation on a fringe. Co-ordinate the four colors
with your favorite coat and bag or consider using yarns of one color but of different
textures for a subtle look. Designed by Luise Roberts.*

Materials

Yarn

Cashmerino Aran by Debbie Bliss, 1¾oz/50g ball,
  each approx 98 yd/90 m (55% merino wool,
  33% microfiber, 12% cashmere)
2 balls in Red 610 (A)
4 balls in blue 208 (C)
Kid Classic by Rowan, 1¾oz/50g ball, each approx
  152 yd/140 m (70% lambswool, 26% kid
  mohair, 4% nylon)
1 ball in Feather 828 (B)
1 ball in Peach Sorbet 842 (D)

Hooks and extras

US 7 (4.50 mm) crochet hook
Tapestry needle

Gauge

Work a Small Motif, which should be 3 in.
  (7½ cm) square. Change hook size, if necessary,
  to obtain this gauge.

Sizes and Measurements

Actual measurements: 10 × 75 in. (27 × 190 cm)

Small Motif (Make 36)

Using A, ch 5, join with ss to form a ring.
Crochet over the yarn ends as you work to reduce
the number of ends to weave in at the end.

Round 1: 3 ch (count as 1 dc), 2 dc into ring, [3 ch,
3 dc into ring] 3 times, 3 ch, ss into top of 3 ch.
Cut and finish off A.
Join in B at a ch sp but not at the point where round
1 starts and finishes.

Round 2: 3 ch (count as 1 dc) 2 dc into the ch sp, 3
ch, 3 dc into same ch sp, *2 ch, [3 dc, 3 ch, 3 dc]
into next ch sp; rep from * twice more, 2 ch, ss into
top of 3 ch.
Cut and finish off B.
Join in C at a side 2 ch sp.

Round 3: 3 ch (count as 1 dc) 2 dc into the ch sp, *2
ch, [3 dc, 3 ch, 3 dc] into corner 3 ch sp, 2 ch, 3 dc
into the next ch sp; rep from * twice more, 2 ch, [3
dc, 3 ch, 3 dc] into corner 3 ch sp, 2 ch, ss into the
top of 3 ch.
Cut and finish off C.
Join in D in the back loop of a side st.

Round 4: *ss into the back loop of each st until each
corner ch st, 1 ch, 1 ss into the corner st, 1 ch; rep
from * 3 times, ss into back loop of each st.

Cut and finish off D, weaving the end tail around the first st to create a continuous chain. Do not weave in the ends.**

Large Motif (Make 3)
Work rounds 1–3 as for Small Motif.
Cont in the patt set with the foll color sequence.
Round 4: C.
Round 5: A.
Round 6: B.
Round 7: D.
Rounds 8–10: C.
Cut and finish off yarn C.
Join in yarn D in the back loop of a side st.
Round 11: As round 4 of Small Motif to **.

Finishing
Block and press each motif following the information on the ball bands.
Using the diagram as a guide, crochet the motifs together through the inner stitch loops using D. A missed stitch loop will show so work some loops twice rather than skip a stitch in order to ease longer edges together. The seam at the top of each fringe between each strip is 1 in. (2.5 cm) long.
Weave in the ends through the base of the stitch loops or into the thickness of the seams.

Work edging:
Join in A in the back loop of a side st of the last round of C.
Sc into the back loop of each st of the last round of C until each corner ch st, 1 ch, 1 sc into the corner st, 1 ch. Cont until all the sts are worked.
Cut and finish off A, weaving the end tail around the first st to create a continuous chain.

------------------------------------- Center line

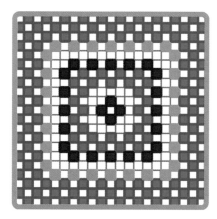

Pendant Bead Necklace

Turn heads with this beautifully simple yet elegant necklace, crocheted with sparkly gold fingering yarn and finished with pendant beads. In this pattern by Sophie Britten, the beads are suspended from the necklace rather than worked into the fabric. If you don't want to make your own pendant beads, look for some that already come in a wire cage with a top loop.

Materials

Yarn

Goldfingering by Twilleys, 1¾oz/50g ball, each
   approx 218 yd/200 m (80% viscose, 20%
   metalized polyester)
1 ball in Turquoise Multicolor Shade 11

Hooks and extras

10 blue glass beads
12 in. (30 cm) length of silver jewelry wire
2 silver jump rings
1 barrel clasp (torpedo clasp)
Pair of round-nosed pliers
3.00 mm crochet hook

Gauge

An exact gauge is not too important for this
   pattern, but you should try to keep your work
   fairly tight.

Sizes and Measurements

To fit: one size
Actual measurement: length 14½ in. (37 cm);
depth excluding beads 1⅜ in. (3.5 cm)

Pendant beads

For each bead, cut a piece of wire approx 1¼ in.
(3 cm) in length. Using round-nosed pliers, make a
small loop at one end to ensure the bead does not
slip off. Thread the bead onto the wire and make a
slightly larger loop at the other end for the yarn to
pass through, pushing the end of the wire back
through the bead.

Thread all the beads onto the yarn before you start.

Necklace

Ch 99.
Row 1 (RS): 1 dc into 4th ch from hook, 1 dc into
each ch to end, turn: 97 sts.
Row 2: 1 ch, 1 sc into each of first 3 dc, *2 ch, skip
1 dc, [2 dc, 2 ch] twice into next dc, skip 1 dc, 1 sc
into each of next 5 dc; rep from * omitting 2 sc at
end of last rep and placing last sc into top of 3 ch,
turn.
Row 3: 1 ch, 1 sc into each of first 2 sc, *3 ch, skip
next 2 ch sp, (3 dc, 2 ch, 3 dc) into next 2 ch sp, 3

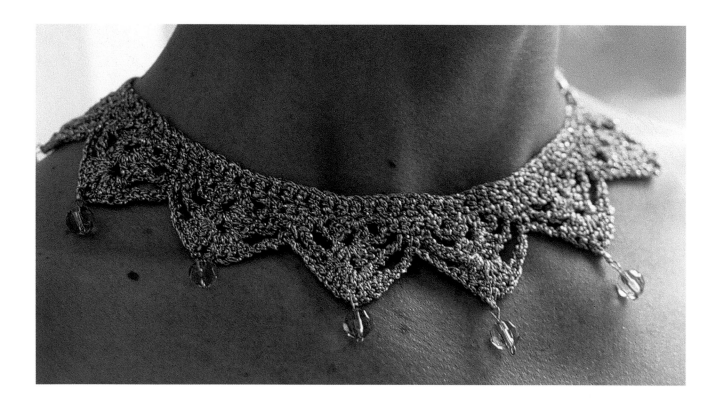

ch, skip 1 sc, 1 sc into each of next 3 sc; rep from * to end, omitting 1 sc at end of last rep, turn.

Row 4: 1 ch, 1 sc into first sc, 4 ch, skip next 3 ch sp, (4 dc, 2 ch, 4 dc) into next 2 ch sp, 4 ch, skip 1 sc, 1 sc into next sc, *4 ch, skip next 3 ch sp, (4 dc, 1 ch, slide up a bead, 1 ch, 4 dc) into next 2 ch sp, 4 ch, skip 1 sc, 1 sc into next sc; rep from * to end. Note that the last rep will not carry a bead. Fasten off.

Finishing

Firmly press the fabric, avoiding the beads. Attach each half of the clasp to a jump ring and fasten the rings to each end of the first row.

Neck High

If you cannot find a suitable clasp you can crochet a single chain at each end of the necklace to tie it at the back, following the instructions to be found on page 78.

Another alternative fixing method is to stitch a small hook and eye to each end of the necklace, but this will not offer such a secure fastening as the barrel clasp.

The design of this necklace is based on a crochet edging pattern so you could adapt any of the edgings on pages 168–169 for a different look. Twilley's Goldfingering comes in a range of 19 colors and five multicolors, so you can easily make a necklace to match every outfit!

If you cannot find this yarn, Lion Brand Lamé is a good substitute.

Leg Warmers

Keep cozy in the cold with ultra chic and comfy leg warmers. Created by Sue Whiting, they're worked in a mock rib made up of relief doubles for a jolt of texture. The variegated effect is all in the yarn.

Materials

Yarn
Freedom Spirit by Twilleys, 1¾oz/50g ball, each
approx 55 yd/50 m (100% wool)
6 balls in Soul 501

Hooks and extras
H/8 (5.00 mm) crochet hook

Gauge
15 sts and 10 rounds to 4 in. (10 cm) measured
over pattern using H/8 (5.00 mm) hook. Change
hook size, if necessary, to obtain this gauge.

Special Abbreviations
rbdc = relief back double worked as follows: work
a double in the usual way but working st around
stem of st of previous round, inserting hook from
right to left and from back to front around stem
of this st. Also called bpdc, or back post double
crochet.
rfdc = relief front double worked as follows: work
a double in the usual way but working st around
stem of st of previous round, inserting hook from
right to left and from front to back around stem
of this st. Also called fpdc, or front post double
crochet.

Sizes and Measurements
To fit: average size ladies leg
Actual measurements: width at ankle 10½ in.
(27 cm); **width at top** 15¾ in. (40 cm); **length
(excluding turn-back)** 14 in. (36 cm)

Leg warmers (Make two the same)
Ch 40 and join with a ss to form a ring.
Round 1 (RS): 2 ch (counts as first hdc), skip ch at
base of 2 ch, 1 hdc into each ch to end, ss to top of
2 ch at beg of round: 40 sts.

Round 2: 2 ch (count as first st), *1 rbdc around
stem of next st**, 1 rfdc around stem of next st, rep
from * to end, ending last rep at **, ss to top of 2 ch
at beg of round.
Round 3: 2 ch (count as first st), 1 hdc into st at base
of 2 ch—1 st increased, *1 rbdc around stem of next
st**, 1 rfdc around stem of next st, rep from * to
end, ending last rep at **, 1 hdc into st at base of 2
ch at beg of round—1 st increased, ss to top of 2 ch
at beg of round: 42 sts.

Round 4: 2 ch (count as first st), *1 rfdc around stem of next st**, 1 rbdc around stem of next st, rep from * to end, ending last rep at **, ss to top of 2 ch at beg of round.

Round 5: As round 4.

Round 6: 2 ch (count as first st), 1 hdc into st at base of 2 ch—1 st increased, *1 rfdc around stem of next st**, 1 rbdc around stem of next st, rep from * to end, ending last rep at **, 1 hdc into st at base of 2 ch at beg of round—1 st increased, ss to top of 2 ch at beg of round: 44 sts.

Round 7: As round 2.

Rounds 8 to 31: As rounds 2 to 7, 4 times: 60 sts.

Round 32: As round 2.

Rep last round until leg warmer measures 18¾ in. (48 cm)

Fasten off.

Finishing

Do NOT press. Fold last 12 rounds to outside around upper edge to form turn-back.

One Leg Up

These great leg warmers are worked in the round, so there is no sewing up to be done at the end—just fasten off and you are ready to go.

Remember that when working in the round, you still need to start each round by making a chain to the height of the stitch you are using (in this case half double crochet, so you make 2 ch) and finish by joining with a slip stitch so that you are working a complete round each time. If you were to just keep working around continuously you would end up with a flat spiral that has no joins but does have a step at the end. This is great for some projects, such as coasters, but would not work well with this one.

The multi-colored effect in these leg warmers is created by the yarn itself—there is no need for any change in yarn to create the subtle color design. However, you could create brightly striped leg warmers by changing the color of yarn used every few rounds. Have fun and experiment to see what width stripe works the best!

Sue Whiting has designed these leg warmers to have a stylish turn back at the top, but you can also wear them without the turn back, with the excess length gently gathered around the ankle—as in our photograph—for a more casual look.

Rose-Top Hairsticks

*Jazz up some plain hairsticks in minutes with these really easy roses
designed by Sophie Britten. They are worked in a long strip and wound around the
stick to create a bud and finished with a band of satin or velvet ribbon.*

Materials

Yarn
Goldfingering by Twilleys, 1¾oz/50g ball, each
   approx 218 yd/200 m (80% viscose, 20%
   metalized polyester)
1 ball in Sea Green 66
1 ball in Black 31

Hooks and extras
2.50 mm crochet hook
1 pair of wooden hairsticks
1 pair of plastic hairsticks
4 in. (10 cm) of ¼ in. (0.5 cm) wide light green
   satin ribbon
4 in. (10 cm) of ⅝ in. (1.5 cm) wide black velvet
   ribbon
Strong craft glue
2 sequins
2 seed beads

Gauge
Exact gauge is not too important for this pattern,
   but you should keep your work fairly tight.

Special Abbreviations
V-stitch =1 dc, 1 ch, 1 dc

Rose
Ch 35.
Row 1: Work 1 dc into 5th ch from hook, *1 ch, skip
1 ch, work 1 V-stitch into next ch; rep from * to end,
turn.
Row 2: 3 ch (count as 1 dc), 5dc into ch sp at center
of first V-stitch, *1 dc into next ch sp, 6 dc into ch sp
at center of next V-stitch; rep from *
to end.
Fasten off, leaving a 4 in. (10 cm) tail.

Finishing
Put a dab of glue around the top of the hairstick and
glue one end of the rose in place. Now wind the rest
of the rose around the hairstick and secure with a
dab of glue. Weave the tail through the petals to
secure firmly. Fasten off and sew in ends.

Place a dab of glue around the hairstick beneath the
rose and take a length of ribbon just enough to reach
around the hairstick with a small overlap and secure
with glue.

Place a dab of glue on top of the hairstick, then place
a sequin on top, with a seed bead in the center to
finish.

Beaded Bag

*This glamorous little beaded bag combines a glittery Lurex yarn with
sparkly glass beads to make the perfect little purse for big nights out. You can
either match the beads to the yarn, as designer Sue Whiting has done, for a subtle sparkle
or use a different color for a rather more jazzy effect.*

Materials

Yarn
Goldfingering by Twilleys, 1¾oz/50g ball, each
approx 218 yd/200 m (80% viscose, 20%
metalized polyester)
4 balls in Peacock Blue 63

Hooks and extras
2.50 mm crochet hook
Approx 2,260 turquoise glass beads

Gauge
24 sts and 27 rows to 4 in. (10 cm) measured over
beaded pattern using 2.50 mm hook. Change
hook size, if necessary, to obtain this gauge.

Special Abbreviations
beaded ch = slide bead up next to work, yo and
draw loop through leaving bead sitting against
RS of work
beaded sc = insert hook as indicated, slide bead
up next to work, yo and draw loop through
leaving bead sitting against RS of work, yo and
draw through both loops on hook.

Bead it!
Before starting to crochet all sections except
Gusset, you will need to thread the beads onto
yarn. See page 44 for instructions.

While working the patt, the beaded ch do NOT
count as sts. When working across top of foll
rows, skip the beaded ch and only work into the
sc of previous rows. Ensure all beads sit on RS of
work by gently easing them through to that side
of the work.

Actual measurements: width 8 in. (23 cm);
height (to opening edge) 4¾ in. (12 cm)

Sides (Make 2)
Thread approx 650 beads onto yarn.
With 2.50 mm hook, ch 43.
Row 1 (RS): 1 sc into 2nd ch from hook, 1 sc into
each ch to end, turn: 42 sts.
Row 2: 1 ch (does NOT count as st), 2 sc into first sc,
*1 beaded ch, 1 sc into each of next 2 sc, rep from *
to last st, 1 beaded ch, 2 sc into last sc, turn: 44 sts.
Rows 3 to 5: As row 2: 50 sts.
Row 6: 1 ch (does NOT count as st), 1 sc into first sc,
*1 beaded ch, 1 sc into each of next 2 sc, rep from *
to last st, 1 beaded ch, 1 sc into last sc, turn.
Row 7: 1 ch (does NOT count as st), 2 sc into first sc,

1 sc into next sc, *1 beaded ch, 1 sc into each of next 2 sc, rep from * to last 2 sts, 1 beaded ch, 1 sc into next sc, 2 sc into last sc, turn: 52 sts.

Row 8: 1 ch (does NOT count as st), 1 sc into each of first 2 sc, *1 beaded ch, 1 sc into each of next 2 sc, rep from * to end, turn.

Row 9: As row 2: 54 sts.

Row 10: As row 6.

Row 11: As row 8.

Rep last 2 rows 3 times more.

Row 18: As row 6.

Row 19: 1 ch (does NOT count as st), sc2tog over first 2 sts, *1 beaded ch, 1 sc into each of next 2 sc, rep from * to last 2 sts, 1 beaded ch, sc2tog over last 2 sts, turn: 52 sts.

Row 20: As row 8.

Rows 21 and 22: As rows 10 and 11.

Row 23: 1 ch (does NOT count as st), sc2tog over

first 2 sts, 1 sc into next sc, *1 beaded ch, 1 sc into each of next 2 sc, rep from * to last 3 sts, 1 beaded ch, 1 sc into next sc, sc2tog over last 2 sts, turn: 50 sts.

Rows 24 and 25: As rows 10 and 11.

Row 26: As row 6.

Row 27: As row 19: 48 sts.

Row 28: As row 8.

Row 29: As row 6.

Row 30: As row 19: 46 sts.

Row 31: As row 8.

Row 32: As row 6.

Shape upper edge:

Row 33 (RS): 1 ch (does NOT count as st), sc2tog over first 2 sts, [1 beaded ch, 1 sc into each of next 2 sc] 6 times, 1 beaded ch, 1 sc into next sc and turn, leaving rem sts unworked: 14 sts.

Work on these sts only for first side.

Row 34: 1 ch (does NOT count as st), sc2tog over first 2 sts, *1 beaded ch, 1 sc into each of next 2 sc, rep from * to end, turn: 13 sts.

Row 35: 1 ch (does NOT count as st), sc2tog over first 2 sts, 1 sc into next sc, *1 beaded ch, 1 sc into each of next 2 sc, rep from * to last 2 sts, 1 beaded ch, sc2tog over last 2 sts, turn: 11 sts.

Row 36: 1 ch (does NOT count as st), sc2tog over first 2 sts, *1 beaded ch, 1 sc into each of next 2 sc, rep from * to last st, 1 sc into last st, turn: 10 sts.

Row 37: 1 ch (does NOT count as st), sc2tog over first 2 sts, *1 beaded ch, 1 sc into each of next 2 sc, rep from * to last 2 sts, 1 beaded ch, sc2tog over last 2 sts, turn: 8 sts.

Row 38: 1 ch (does NOT count as st), sc2tog over first 2 sts, *1 beaded ch, 1 sc into each of next 2 sc, rep from * to end, turn: 7 sts.

Row 39: 1 ch (does NOT count as st), sc2tog over first 2 sts, 1 sc into next sc, 1 beaded ch, 1 sc into each of next 2 sc, 1 beaded ch, sc2tog over last 2 sts, turn: 5 sts.

Row 40: 1 ch (does NOT count as st), 1 sc into each of first 2 sts, 1 beaded ch, 1 sc into each of next 2 sc, 1 beaded ch, 1 sc into last st, turn.

Row 41: 1 ch (does NOT count as st), sc2tog over first 2 sts, 1 beaded ch, 1 sc into next sc, sc2tog over last 2 sts, turn: 3 sts.

Row 42: 1 ch (does NOT count as st), 1 sc into first st, 1 beaded ch, 1 sc into each of last 2 sc, turn.

Row 43: 1 ch (does NOT count as st), sc2tog over first 2 sts, 1 sc into last sc, turn: 2 sts.

Row 44: 1 ch (does NOT count as st), 1 sc into each of next 2 sc.
Fasten off.

Return to last complete row worked, skip center 16 sc (and 9 beaded ch), rejoin yarn to next sc and cont as follows:

Row 33 (RS): 1 ch (does NOT count as st), 1 sc into same sc as where yarn was re-joined, [1 beaded ch, 1 sc into each of next 2 sc] 6 times, 1 beaded ch, sc2tog over last 2 sts, turn: 14 sts.

Row 34: 1 ch (does NOT count as st), 1 sc into each of first 2 sc, *1 beaded ch, 1 sc into each of next 2 sc, rep from * to last 2 sts, 1 beaded ch, sc2tog over last 2 sts, turn: 13 sts.

Row 35: 1 ch (does NOT count as st), sc2tog over first 2 sts, *1 beaded ch, 1 sc into each of next 2 sc, rep from * to last 3 sts, 1 beaded ch, 1 sc into next sc, sc2tog over last 2 sts, turn: 11 sts.

Row 36: 1 ch (does NOT count as st), 1 sc into first st, *1 beaded ch, 1 sc into each of next 2 sc, rep from * to last 2 sts, 1 beaded ch, sc2tog over last 2 sts, turn: 10 sts.

Row 37: 1 ch (does NOT count as st), sc2tog over first 2 sts, *1 beaded ch, 1 sc into each of next 2 sc, rep from * to last 2 sts, 1 beaded ch, sc2tog over last 2 sts, turn: 8 sts.

Row 38: 1 ch (does NOT count as st), 1 sc into each of first 2 sc, *1 beaded ch, 1 sc into each of next 2 sc, rep from * to last 2 sts, 1 beaded ch, sc2tog over

last 2 sts, turn: 7 sts.

Row 39: 1 ch (does NOT count as st), sc2tog over first 2 sts, 1 beaded ch, 1 sc into each of next 2 sc, 1 beaded ch, 1 sc into next sc, sc2tog over last 2 sts, turn: 5 sts.

Row 40: 1 ch (does NOT count as st), 1 sc into first st, 1 beaded ch, 1 sc into each of next 2 sc, 1 beaded ch, 1 sc into each of last 2 sts, turn.

Row 41: 1 ch (does NOT count as st), sc2tog over first 2 sts, 1 sc into next sc, 1 beaded ch, sc2tog over last 2 sts, turn: 3 sts.

Row 42: 1 ch (does NOT count as st), 1 sc into each of first 2 sts, 1 beaded ch, 1 sc into last st, turn.

Row 43: 1 ch (does NOT count as st), 1 sc into first sc, sc2tog over last 2 sts, turn: 2 sts.

Row 44: 1 ch (does NOT count as st), 1 sc into each of next 2 sc.
Fasten off.

Gusset
Place marker at center point of foundation ch edge of one side.

Work First Section:
With 2.50 mm hook, ch 11.

Row 1 (RS): 1 sc into 2nd ch from hook, 1 sc into each ch to end, turn: 10 sts.

Row 2: 1 ch (does NOT count as st), 1 sc into each sc to end, turn.

Rows 3 to 44: As row 2.

Row 45: 1 ch (does NOT count as st), sc2tog over first 2 sts, 1 sc into each sc to last 2 sts, sc2tog over last 2 sts, turn: 8 sts.

Rows 46 to 52: As row 2.

Row 53: As row 45: 6 sts.

Rows 54 to 60: As row 2.

Row 61: As row 45: 4 sts.

Rows 62 to 66: As row 2.

Row 67: 1 ch (does NOT count as st), sc2tog over first 2 sts, sc2tog over last 2 sts, turn: 2 sts.

Now rep row 2 until row-end edge of Gusset fits from marker on foundation ch edge of Side, along foundation ch edge and up shaped row-end edge to top of last row.
Fasten off.

Work Second Section:
With RS facing, rejoin yarn to first ch of foundation ch edge of first section, 1 ch (does NOT count as st), 1 sc into each foundation ch of First Section, turn: 10 sts.
Complete Second Section to match First Section from row 2 onwards.

Finishing
Do NOT press.

Work opening edge edging
Thread approx 40 beads onto yarn.
With RS facing and 2.50 mm hook, rejoin yarn at beg of last row worked of first side of Side and work along shaped opening edge as follows: 1 ch (does NOT count as st), work 1 row of sc evenly along opening edge to fasten-off point of second side, turn.
Next row (WS): 1 ch (does NOT count as st), 1 sc into first sc, 1 beaded sc into each sc to last sc, 1 sc into last sc.
Fasten off.
Work the edging on the other Side in same way.

Matching tops of last rows worked on each section and foundation ch edge of Gusset First Section to marker on foundation ch edge of Side, pin and tack Gusset to foundation ch and row end edges of Side.

Make side edging
Thread approx 140 beads onto yarn.
With RS of Side piece facing and using 2.50 mm hook, attach yarn at beg of last row of second side

of Side and, working each st through both Side and Gusset, work around outer edge of Side as follows: 1 ch (does NOT count as st), work 1 row of sc evenly around entire outer edge, ending at fasten-off point of first side of Side, turn.
Next row (WS): 1 ch (does NOT count as st), 1 sc into first sc, 1 beaded sc into each sc to last sc, 1 sc into last sc.
Join other Side to remaining row-end edge of Gusset in same way.

Handle
Thread approx 600 beads onto yarn.
With 2.50 mm hook, ch 8 and join with a ss to form a ring.
Round 1 (WS): 1 ch (does not count as st), 1 sc into each ch to end: 8 sts.
Round 2: 1 beaded sc into each st to end.
Cont in spiraling rounds of beaded sc until Handle measures 11¾ in. (30 cm).
Next round: 1 sc into each st to end, ss to next st.
Fasten off.

Sew ends of Handle securely to top edges of Sides and Gusset as in photograph.

Cozy & Comfy Mittens

Designed by Sue Whiting, these clever mittens have simple rows of popcorns down the back of the hand to provide extra textual interest. Made in rounds using a wool and cotton blend yarn, they grow quickly and there are no seams to sew up afterwards.

Materials

Yarn
Wool Cotton by Rowan, 1¾oz/50g ball, each
   approx 123 yd/113 m (50% wool, 50% cotton)
2 balls in Citron 901

Hooks and extras
E/4 (3.50 mm) crochet hook

Gauge
17 sts and 16 rows to 4 in. (10 cm) measured over
   pattern using E/4 (3.50 mm) hook. Change hook
   size, if necessary, to obtain this gauge.

Special Abbreviations
Popcorn = work 5 dc as indicated, remove hook
   from working loop, insert it through both strands
   at top of first of these 5 dc just made, replace
   working loop on hook and draw through first dc.
hdc2tog = [yo, insert hook as indicated, yo and
   draw loop through] twice, yo and draw through
   all 5 loops.

Sizes and Measurements
To fit: average size lady's hand
Actual measurements: width around hand 7¾
in. (20 cm); **length** 18½ in. (22 cm)

95

Right Mitten

Ch 34 and join with a ss to form a ring.

Round 1 (RS): 1 ch (does NOT count as st), 1 sc into each ch to end, ss to first sc, turn: 34 sts.

Round 2: 1 ch (does NOT count as st), 1 sc into each sc to end, ss to first sc, turn.

Rounds 3 and 4: As round 2.

Round 5: 2 ch (counts as first hdc), skip sc at base of 2 ch, 1 hdc into each of next 5 sc, 1 popcorn into next sc, 1 hdc into each of next 3 sc, 1 popcorn into next sc, 1 hdc into each of last 23 sc, ss to top of 2 ch at beg of round, turn.

Cont in patt.

Round 6 (WS): Ss between hdc at end and 2 ch at beg of last round, 2 ch (counts as first hdc), *skip next st (a hdc or popcorn), 1 hdc between st just skipped and next st, rep from * to end, ss to top of 2 ch at beg of round, turn.

Round 7: Ss between hdc at end and 2 ch at beg of last round, 2 ch (counts as first hdc), [skip next st, 1 hdc between st just skipped and next st] 5 times, skip next st, 1 popcorn between st just skipped and next st, [skip next st, 1 hdc between st just skipped and next st] 3 times, skip next st, 1 popcorn between st just skipped and next st, *skip next st, 1 hdc between st just skipped and next st, rep from * to end, ss to top of 2 ch at beg of round, turn.

Rounds 6 and 7 form patt.

Work patt for further 10 rounds, ending on RS round.

Shape thumb hole:

Round 18 (WS): Ss between hdc at end and 2 ch at beg of last round, 2 ch (counts as first hdc), [skip next st, 1 hdc between st just skipped and next st] 11 times, 5 ch, skip next 6 sts, 1 hdc between last st skipped and next st, *skip next st, 1 hdc between st just skipped and next st, rep from * to end, ss to top of 2 ch at beg of round, turn.

Round 19: Ss between hdc at end and 2 ch at beg of last round, 2 ch (counts as first hdc), [skip next st, 1

hdc between st just skipped and next st] 5 times, skip next st, 1 popcorn between st just skipped and next st, [skip next st, 1 hdc between st just skipped and next st] 3 times, skip next st, 1 popcorn between st just skipped and next st, [skip next st, 1 hdc between st just skipped and next st] 6 times, 1 hdc into each of next 5 ch, 1 hdc into ch sp, [skip next st, 1 hdc between st just skipped and next st] 11 times, ss to top of 2 ch at beg of round, turn.

Work patt for further 15 rounds, ending on WS round.

Shape top:

Round 35 (RS): Ss between hdc at end and 2 ch at beg of last round, 2 ch (does NOT count as st), [skip next st, 1 hdc between st just skipped and next st] 5 times, skip next st, 1 popcorn between st just skipped and next st, [skip next st, 1 hdc between st just skipped and next st] 3 times, skip next st, 1 popcorn between st just skipped and next st, [skip next st, 1 hdc between st just skipped and next st] 4 times, [hdc2tog] twice, [skip next st, 1 hdc between st just skipped and next st] 13 times, hdc2tog, ss to top of first hdc at beg of round, turn: 30 sts.

Round 36: Ss between hdc2tog at end and hdc at beg of last round, 2 ch (counts as first hdc), *skip next st (a hdc, hdc2tog or popcorn), 1 hdc between st just skipped and next st, rep from * to end, ss to top of 2 ch at beg of round, turn.

Round 37: Ss between hdc at end and 2 ch at beg of last round, 2 ch (does NOT count as st), [skip next st, 1 hdc between st just skipped and next st] 4 times, skip next st, 1 popcorn between st just skipped and next st, [skip next st, 1 hdc between st just skipped and next st] 3 times, skip next st, 1 popcorn between st just skipped and next st, [skip next st, 1 hdc between st just skipped and next st] 3 times, [hdc2tog] twice, [skip next st, 1 hdc between st just skipped and next st] 11 times, hdc2tog, ss to top of first hdc at beg of round, turn: 26 sts.

Round 38: As round 36.

Round 39: Ss between hdc at end and 2 ch at beg of last round, 2 ch (does NOT count as st), [skip next st, 1 hdc between st just skipped and next st] 3 times, skip next st, 1 popcorn between st just skipped and next st, [skip next st, 1 hdc between st just skipped and next st] 3 times, skip next st, 1 popcorn between st just skipped and next st, [skip next st, 1 hdc between st just skipped and next st] twice, [hdc2tog] twice, [skip next st, 1 hdc between st just skipped and next st] 9 times, hdc2tog, ss to top of first hdc at beg of round, turn: 22 sts.

Round 40: Ss between hdc at end and 2 ch at beg of last round, 2 ch (does NOT count as st), [skip next st, 1 hdc between st just skipped and next st] 8 times, [hdc2tog] twice, [skip next st, 1 hdc between st just skipped and next st] 7 times, hdc2tog, ss to top of first hdc at beg of round: 18 sts.

Turn Mitten inside out, so that RS are facing and fold flat. Close top of Mitten by working a row of sc through top of sts of both layers.
Fasten off.

Shape thumb:

With RS facing, rejoin yarn to 3rd of 5 ch of round 18 at base of thumb opening and work around thumb opening.

Round 1 (RS): 2 ch (counts as first hdc), 1 hdc into each of next 2 ch, 1 hdc into side of hdc of round 18 at side of thumb opening, 1 hdc into each of the 5 sps between hdc across top of round 17, 1 hdc into side of hdc of 18th round at other side of thumb opening, 1 hdc into each of next 2 ch of round 18, ss to top of 2 ch at beg of round, turn: 12 sts.

Round 2: Ss between hdc at end and 2 ch at beg of last round, 2 ch (counts as first hdc), *skip next st, 1 hdc between st just skipped and next st, rep from * to end, ss to top of 2 ch at beg of round, turn.

Rounds 3 to 8: As round 2.

Round 9: Ss between hdc at end and 2 ch at beg of last round, 2 ch (does NOT count as st), skip next st, 1

hdc between st just skipped and next st, [hdc2tog] 5 times, ss to top of first hdc at beg of round, turn: 6 sts.

Round 10: 1 ch (does NOT count as st), working between sts of previous round as in previous rounds: [sc2tog] 3 times, ss to first sc2tog.
Fasten off.

Left Mitten

Work as for Right Mitten to end of 4th round.

Round 5: 2 ch (counts as first hdc), skip sc at base of 2 ch, 1 hdc into each of next 22 sc, 1 popcorn into next sc, 1 hdc into each of next 3 sc, 1 popcorn into next sc, 1 hdc into each of last 6 sc, ss to top of 2 ch at beg of round, turn.
Cont in patt.

Round 6 (WS): Ss between hdc at end and 2 ch at beg of last round, 2 ch (counts as first hdc), *skip next st (a hdc or popcorn), 1 hdc between st just skipped and next st, rep from * to end, ss to top of 2 ch at beg of round, turn.

Round 7: Ss between hdc at end and 2 ch at beg of last round, 2 ch (counts as first hdc), [skip next st, 1 hdc between st just skipped and next st] 22 times, skip next st, 1 popcorn between st just skipped and next st, [skip next st, 1 hdc between st just skipped and next st] 3 times, skip next st, 1 popcorn between st just skipped and next st, *skip next st, 1 hdc between st just skipped and next st, rep from * to end, ss to top of 2 ch at beg of round, turn.
Rounds 6 and 7 form patt.
Work patt for further 10 rounds, ending on RS round.

Shape thumb hole:

Round 18 (WS): Ss between hdc at end and 2 ch at beg of last round, 2 ch (counts as first hdc), [skip next st, 1 hdc between st just skipped and next st] 16 times, 5 ch, skip next 6 sts, 1 hdc between last st skipped and next st, *skip next st, 1 hdc between st

just skipped and next st, rep from * to end, ss to top of 2 ch at beg of round, turn.

Round 19: Ss between hdc at end and 2 ch at beg of last round, 2 ch (counts as first hdc), [skip next st, 1 hdc between st just skipped and next st] 11 times, 1 hdc into each of next 5 ch, 1 hdc into ch sp, [skip next st, 1 hdc between st just skipped and next st] 5 times, skip next st, 1 popcorn between st just skipped and next st, [skip next st, 1 hdc between st just skipped and next st] 3 times, skip next st, 1 popcorn between st just skipped and next st, [skip next st, 1 hdc between st just skipped and next st] 6 times, ss to top of 2 ch at beg of round, turn.

Work patt for further 15 rounds, ending on WS round.

Shape top:

Round 35 (RS): Ss between hdc at end and 2 ch at beg of last round, 2 ch (does NOT count as st), [skip next st, 1 hdc between st just skipped and next st] 14 times, [hdc2tog] twice, [skip next st, 1 hdc between st just skipped and next st] 4 times, skip next st, 1 popcorn between st just skipped and next st, [skip next st, 1 hdc between st just skipped and next st] 3 times, skip next st, 1 popcorn between st just skipped and next st, [skip next st, 1 hdc between st just skipped and next st] 4 times, hdc2tog, ss to top of first hdc at beg of round, turn: 30 sts.

Round 36: Ss between hdc2tog at end and 2 ch at beg of last round, 2 ch (counts as first hdc), *skip next st (a hdc, hdc2tog or popcorn), 1 hdc between st just skipped and next st, rep from * to end, ss to top of 2 ch at beg of round, turn.

Round 37: Ss between hdc at end and 2 ch at beg of last round, 2 ch (does NOT count as st), [skip next st, 1 hdc between st just skipped and next st] 12 times, [hdc2tog] twice, [skip next st, 1 hdc between st just skipped and next st] 3 times, skip next st, 1 popcorn between st just skipped and next st, [skip next st, 1 hdc between st just skipped and next st] 3 times, skip next st, 1 popcorn between st just skipped and next

st, [skip next st, 1 hdc between st just skipped and next st] 3 times, hdc2tog, ss to top of first hdc at beg of round, turn: 26 sts.

Round 38: As round 36.

Round 39: Ss between hdc at end and 2 ch at beg of last round, 2 ch (does NOT count as st), [skip next st, 1 hdc between st just skipped and next st] 10 times, [hdc2tog] twice, [skip next st, 1 hdc between st just skipped and next st] twice, skip next st, 1 popcorn between st just skipped and next st, [skip next st, 1 hdc between st just skipped and next st] 3 times, skip next st, 1 popcorn between st just skipped and next st, [skip next st, 1 hdc between st just skipped and next st] twice, hdc2tog, ss to top of first hdc at beg of round, turn: 22 sts.

Round 40: Ss between hdc at end and 2 ch at beg of last round, 2 ch (does NOT count as st), [skip next st, 1 hdc between st just skipped and next st] 8 times, [hdc2tog] twice, [skip next st, 1 hdc between st just skipped and next st] 7 times, hdc2tog, ss to top of first hdc at beg of round: 18 sts.

Turn Mitten inside out, RS facing. Close top by working row of sc through top of sts of both layers. Fasten off.

Shape thumb
Work as for Thumb of Right Mitten.

Finishing
Press carefully taking care not to squash popcorns.

Beanie Hats

*Sue Whiting's beanie hats are suitable for a woman or a man—the design is
exactly the same for both, but the man's hat is a little larger. The pattern is worked
quite loosely, as the denim yarn shrinks quite a lot when it is washed.*

Materials

Yarn

Denim by Rowan, 1¾oz/50g ball, each approx
101 yd/93 m (100% cotton)
2 (2) balls in either Nashville 225 or Memphis 229

Hooks and extras

E/4 (3.50 mm) crochet hook
US 6 (4.00 mm) crochet hook

Gauge

Before washing: 18 sts to 4 in. (10 cm) measured
over pattern using US 6 (4.00 mm) hook. First 11
rounds measure 4¾ in. (12 cm). Change hook
size, if necessary, to obtain this gauge.

Special Abbreviations

dc3tog = yo and insert hook into st at base of 3 ch
just worked, yo and draw loop through, yo and
draw through 2 loops, yo, skip 2 sts and insert
hook into next st, yo and draw loop through, yo
and draw through 2 loops, yo and insert hook
into work in same place as last inserted, yo and
draw loop through, yo and draw through 2 loops,
yo and draw through all 4 loops on hook

cluster = *yo and insert hook into same place as
used for last "leg" of previous cluster (or dc3tog
at beg of round), yo and draw loop through, yo
and draw through 2 loops, rep from * once more
inserting hook in same place as before, skip 2
sts, **yo and insert hook into next st, yo and
draw loop through, yo and draw through 2
loops, rep from ** once more inserting hook in
same place as before, yo and draw through all 5
loops on hook

rbdc = relief back double worked as follows: work
a double in the usual way but working around
stem of st of previous row, inserting hook from
back to front and from right to left. Also called
BPdc, or back post double crochet.

rfdc = relief front double worked as follows: work
a double in the usual way but working around
stem of st of previous row, inserting hook from
front to back and from right to left. Also called
FPdc, or front post double crochet.

Hat Trick

Rowan Denim shrinks when washed for the first time. Tension given is before washing, while finished size is after washing. Before Beanie Hat is washed it will appear far too big—but, once washed, it will shrink to the correct size.

Sizes and Measurements

To fit: average size lady's (man's) head

Actual measurements: width around head 20 (21) in. [51 (54) cm]

With US 6 (4.00 mm) hook, ch 96 (102) and join with a ss to form a ring.

Round 1 (RS): 3 ch (does NOT count as st), dc3tog, *2 ch, 1 cluster, rep from * until second half of last cluster has been worked into ch at base of 3 ch at beg of round, 2 ch, ss to dc3tog at beg of round: 96 (102) sts, 32 (34) patt reps.

Round 2: 3 ch (does NOT count as st), dc3tog, *2 ch, 1 cluster, rep from * until second half of last cluster has been worked into ch at base of 3 ch at beg of round, 2 ch, ss to dc3tog at beg of round.

Round 3: As round 2.

Round 4: 2 ch (counts as first hdc), skip dc3tog at base of 2 ch, *2 hdc into next ch sp**, 1 hdc into next cluster, rep from * to end, ending last rep at **, ss to top of 2 ch at beg of round: 96 (102) sts.

Round 5: 2 ch (counts as first st), skip st at base of 2 ch, 1 rbdc around stem of each of next 2 sts, *1 rfdc around stem of each of next 3 sts**, 1 rbdc around stem of each of next 3 sts, rep from * to end, ending last rep at **, ss to top of 2 ch at beg of round: 16 (17) patt rep.

Rounds 6 to 9: As round 5.

Rounds 10 and 11: As round 2. 32 (34) patt reps.

Lady's hat only

Round 12: 3 ch (counts as first dc), skip st at base of 3 ch, *2 dc into next ch sp, 1 dc into next cluster, 1 dc into next ch sp**, 1 dc into next cluster, rep from * to end, ending last rep at **, ss to top of 3 ch at beg of round: 80 sts.

Men's hat only

Round 12: 3 ch (counts as first dc), skip st at base of 3 ch, *2 dc into next ch sp**, 1 dc into next cluster, rep from * to end, ending last rep at **, ss to top of 3 ch at beg of round: 102 sts.

Round 13: 3 ch (counts as first dc), skip st at base of 3 ch, 1 dc into each of next 3 dc, *dc2tog over next 2 dc**, 1 dc into each of next 4 dc, rep from * to end, ending last rep at **, ss to top of 3 ch at beg of round: 85 sts.

Both hats

Shape crown:

Round 1: 3 ch (counts as first dc), skip st at base of 3 ch, 1 dc into each of next 2 dc, *dc2tog over next 2 sts**, 1 dc into each of next 3 dc, rep from * to end, ending last rep at **, ss to top of 3 ch at beg of round: 64 (68) sts.

Round 2: 3 ch (counts as first dc), skip st at base of 3 ch, 1 dc into next dc, *dc2tog over next 2 sts**, 1 dc into each of next 2 dc, rep from * to end, ending last rep at **, ss to top of 3 ch at beg of round: 48 (51) sts.

Round 3: 3 ch (counts as first dc), skip st at base of 3 ch, *dc2tog over next 2 sts**, 1 dc into next dc, rep from * to end, ending last rep at **, ss to top of 3 ch at beg of round: 32 (34) sts.

Round 4: 3 ch (does NOT count as st), skip st at base of 3 ch, 1 dc into next st, [dc2tog over next 2 sts] 15 (16) times, ss to top of dc at beg of round: 16 (17) sts.

Round 5: 3 ch (does NOT count as st), skip st at base of 3 ch, 1 dc into next st, [dc2tog over next 2 sts] 7

times, [1 dc into next st] 0 (1) times, ss to top of dc at beg of round: 8 (9) sts.

Round 6: 1 ch (does NOT count as st), [sc2tog over next 2 sts] 4 times, [1 sc into next st] 0 (1) times: 4 (5) sts.

Round 7: 1 sc into each of next 4 (5) sts.

Round 8: 1 sc into each of next 4 (5) sc.

Round 9: 1 sc into each of next 4 (5) sc, ss to next sc.

Fasten off.

Finishing

Make lower edging:

With RS facing and using 3.50 mm hook, attach yarn to foundation ch edge and work around edge as follows: 1 ch (does NOT count as st), *1 sc into ch at base of cluster, 2 sc into next ch sp, rep from * to end, ss to first sc.

Fasten off.

Machine hot wash and tumble dry beanie hat to shrink it to size.

Home Accents

Add a little panache to your interiors
with the elegant Textured Throw or jazz up the sofa with a
funky Loop-Stitch Cushion—whatever design you choose,
your home will soon be the talk of the town!

Loop-Stitch Cushion

Sophie Britten's wild and wacky cushion front is worked in whorls of sumptuous color-changing yarn, using a loop stitch to give an interesting texture. This is a very easy pattern that produces amazing results and can be made to fit any size cushion.

Materials

Yarn
Point Five by Colinette, 3½oz/100g skein, each
   approx 55 yd/50 m (100% wool)
2 skeins in Fresco

Hooks and extras
M/13 (9 mm) crochet hook
14 × 14 in. (35 × 35 cm) cushion with a loose cover

Gauge
6 sts and 6 rows to 4 in. (10 cm) square measured
   over loop stitch, using a M/13 (9 mm) hook.
   Change hook size, if necessary, to achieve this
   gauge.

Special abbreviations
Loop st = This is a very simple variation on single
   crochet. Insert hook into work as if to work sc,
   pick up the yarn on both sides of the loop made
   by your finger, yo, draw through, yo and draw
   through all loops on hook. (See page 43 for
   steps).

Sizes and Measurements
To fit: 14 × 14 in. (35 × 35 cm) cushion with a
removeable cover.

Cushion front
Ch 25.

Row 1 (RS): 1 dc into 4th ch from hook, 1 dc into
each ch to end, turn: 23 sts.

Row 2: 1 ch, 1 loop st into each dc to end, working
last loop st into top of 3 ch at beg of previous row,
turn.

Row 3: 3 ch, skip 1 st, 1 dc into each st to end, turn.
Rep rows 2 and 3 until work measures 14 in.
(35 cm) ending with a WS row. Fasten off.

Finishing
Remove the cover from the cushion and sew the
crocheted front directly onto the front of the cover.
Replace the cushion into the cover. You can stitch the
front on without removing the cushion first, but be
careful not to stitch through it.

Textured Throw

This lovely home accent is made in two subtle shades of pure cotton yarn to create a slightly mottled effect. Choose colors to compliment your home—or use two strands of the same color. Designed by Sue Whiting, this chunky throw can also be used as a rug.

Materials

Yarn

Handknit Cotton DK by Rowan, 1¾oz/50g ball, each
   approx 92 yd/85 m (100% cotton)
15 balls in Bleached 263
15 balls in Ecru 251

Hooks and extras

H/8 (5.00 mm) crochet hook

Gauge

12 sts and 12 rows to 4 in. (10 cm) over pattern
   using H/8 (5.00 mm) hook and 2 strands of yarn
   held together. Change hook size, if necessary, to
   obtain this gauge.

Special Abbreviations

bobble = make bobble: [yo and insert hook into st,
   yo and draw loop through] 4 times, yo and draw
   through all 9 loops on hook (note: as yarn is
   used double, you will have 9 loops but 18
   strands of yarn on hook)

rbdc = relief back double: work a dc in the usual
   way but working around stem of st, inserting
   hook from back to front and from right to left.
   Also called BPdc, or back post double crochet.

rfdc = relief front double: work a dc in the usual
   way but working around stem of st, inserting
   hook from front to back and from right to left.
   Also called FPdc, or front post double crochet.

Sizes and Measurements

Actual measurements: excluding fringe 29 × 52¾ in. (74 × 134 cm)

Throw

With one strand of each shade of yarn held together (ie 2 strands), ch 86.

Foundation row (RS): 1 sc into 2nd ch from hook, 1 sc into each ch to end, turn: 85 sts.

Next row: 1 ch (does NOT count as st), 1 sc into first sc, [1 rbdc around stem of next sc, 1 sc into next sc, 1 rbdc around stem of next sc, 1 sc into each of next 13 sc] 5 times, [1 rbdc around stem of next sc, 1 sc into next sc] twice, turn.

Cont in patt

Row 1 (RS): 1 ch (does NOT count as st), 1 sc into first sc, 1 rfdc around stem of next rbdc, 1 sc into next sc, 1 rfdc around stem of next rbdc, *1 sc into each of next 6 sc, 1 bobble into next sc, 1 sc into each of next 6 sc, 1 rfdc around stem of next rbdc, 1 sc into next sc, 1 rfdc around stem of next rbdc**, 1 sc into each of next 13 sc, 1 rfdc around stem of next

Have a Ball

A bobble is a cluster of stitches worked in the same place and joined together at the top—unlike those in a popcorn, which are separate stitches folded around and closed.

Bobbles are most effective when the stitches before and after them in the background fabric are short, and they are worked on a wrong side row. They are not as solid as popcorns and can easily be flattened by ironing, so be careful never to iron over the area of bobbles if the rest of the item needs blocking.

This project is worked with two strands of yarn—one in each color—which makes the final throw very thick, firm and chunky.

The two colors of yarn used here are very neutral, but you can chose two toning colors from the color scheme of your room for a throw that will co-ordinate perfectly with your interior. Avoid using colors that are very different to each other, because this design relies on achieving a mottled effect over the entire throw, rather than defined areas of different color.

rbdc, 1 sc into next sc, 1 rfdc around stem of next rbdc; rep from * once more, then from * to ** again, 1 sc into last sc, turn.

Row 2 and every foll alt row: 1 ch (does NOT count as st), 1 sc into first sc, [1 rbdc around stem of next rfdc, 1 sc into next sc, 1 rbdc around stem of next rfdc, 1 sc into each of next 13 sts] 5 times, [1 rbdc around stem of next rfdc, 1 sc into next sc] twice, turn.

Row 3: 1 ch (does NOT count as st), 1 sc into first sc, 1 rfdc around stem of next rbdc, 1 sc into next sc, 1 rfdc around stem of next rbdc, *1 sc into each of next 4 sc, 1 bobble into next sc, 1 sc into each of next 3 sc, 1 bobble into next sc, 1 sc into each of next 4 sc, 1 rfdc around stem of next rbdc, 1 sc into next sc, 1 rfdc around stem of next rbdc**, 1 sc into each of next 13 sc, 1 rfdc around stem of next rbdc, 1 sc into next sc, 1 rfdc around stem of next rbdc; rep from * once more, then from * to ** again, 1 sc into last sc, turn.

Row 5: 1 ch (does NOT count as st), 1 sc into first sc, 1 rfdc around stem of next rbdc, 1 sc into next sc, 1 rfdc around stem of next rbdc, *1 sc into each of next 2 sc, 1 bobble into next sc, 1 sc into each of next 7 sc, 1 bobble into next sc, 1 sc into each of next 2 sc, 1 rfdc around stem of next rbdc, 1 sc into next sc, 1 rfdc around stem of next rbdc**, 1 sc into each of next 13 sc, 1 rfdc around stem of next rbdc, 1 sc into next sc, 1 rfdc around stem of next rbdc; rep from * once more, then from * to ** again, 1 sc into last sc, turn.

Row 7: As row 3.

Row 9: As row 1.

Row 11: 1 ch (does NOT count as st), 1 sc into first sc, 1 rfdc around stem of next rbdc, 1 sc into next sc, 1 rfdc around stem of next rbdc, [1 sc into each of next 13 sc, 1 rfdc around stem of next rbdc, 1 sc into next sc, 1 rfdc around stem of next sc] 5 times, 1 sc into last sc, turn.

Row 13: 1 ch (does NOT count as st), 1 sc into first

sc, 1 rfdc around stem of next rbdc, 1 sc into next sc, 1 rfdc around stem of next rbdc, *1 sc into each of next 13 sc, 1 rfdc around stem of next rbdc, 1 sc into next sc, 1 rfdc around stem of next rbdc**, 1 sc into each of next 6 sc, 1 bobble into next sc, 1 sc into each of next 6 sc, 1 rfdc around stem of next rbdc, 1 sc into next sc, 1 rfdc around stem of next rbdc; rep from * once more, then from * to ** again, 1 sc into last sc, turn.

Row 15: 1 ch (does NOT count as st), 1 sc into first sc, 1 rfdc around stem of next rbdc, 1 sc into next sc, 1 rfdc around stem of next rbdc, *1 sc into each of next 13 sc, 1 rfdc around stem of next rbdc, 1 sc into next sc, 1 rfdc around stem of next rbdc**, 1 sc into each of next 4 sc, 1 bobble into next sc, 1 sc into each of next 3 sc, 1 bobble into next sc, 1 sc into each of next 4 sc, 1 rfdc around stem of next rbdc, 1 sc into next sc, 1 rfdc around stem of next rbdc; rep from * once more, then from * to ** again, 1 sc into last sc, turn.

Row 17: 1 ch (does NOT count as st), 1 sc into first sc, 1 rfdc around stem of next rbdc, 1 sc into next sc, 1 rfdc around stem of next rbdc, *1 sc into each of next 13 sc, 1 rfdc around stem of next rbdc, 1 sc into next sc, 1 rfdc around stem of next rbdc**, 1 sc into each of next 2 sc, 1 bobble into next sc, 1 sc into each of next 7 sc, 1 bobble into next sc, 1 sc into each of next 2 sc, 1 rfdc around stem of next rbdc, 1 sc into next sc, 1 rfdc around stem of next rbdc; rep from * once more, then from * to ** again, 1 sc into last sc, turn.

Row 19: As row 15.

Row 21: As row 13.

Row 23: As row 11.

Row 24: As row 2.

These 24 rows form patt.

Rep last 24 rows 5 times more, then rows 1 to 11 again but do NOT turn at end of last row.

Do NOT fasten off.

Border

With RS facing, work 1 round of sc around entire outer edge, working 3 sc into corners and ending with ss to first sc, do NOT turn.

Now work 1 round of crab st (sc worked from left to right, instead of right to left) around entire outer edge, ending with ss to first sc.

Fasten off.

Finishing

Do NOT press.

Cut 10 in. (25 cm) lengths of yarn and knot groups of 4 of these lengths (2 lengths of each color) through shorter ends of throw to form fringe—place a knot in each corner, then place knots on every other st across ends.

Classic Afghan

*Made up of simple textured motifs that are joined as they are worked,
this vintage inspired throw can be made to fit any size of bed. Feel free to explore
your creativity and create one in your own favorite palette.*

Materials

Yarn

Cotton Glace by Rowan, 1¾oz/50g ball, each
approx 125 yd/115 m (100% cotton)

52 (77) balls in Ecru 725 (A)

7 (11) balls in Zeal 813 (B)

7 (11) balls in Pick & Mix 820 (C)

7 (11) balls in Blood Orange 445 (D)

7 (11) balls in Dijon 739 (E)

Hooks and extras

3.00 mm crochet hook

Gauge

One motif measures 3¼ in. (8 cm) square using
3.00 mm hook. Change hook size, if necessary,
to obtain this gauge.

Special Abbreviations

cluster 3 = [yo and insert hook into st, yo and
draw loop through] 3 times, yo and draw
through all 7 loops on hook

cluster 4 = [yo and insert hook into st, yo and
draw loop through] 4 times, yo and draw
through all 9 loops on hook

Sizes and Measurements

Actual measurements: single bedspread 67¼ ×
98¾ in. (171 × 251 cm); **double bedspread** 98¾ ×
98¾ in. (251 × 251 cm)

Basic motif

With 3.00 mm hook and one of the center colors, ch
6 and join with a ss to form a ring.

Round 1 (RS): 5 ch (counts as 1 dc and 2 ch), [1 dc
into ring, 2 ch] 7 times, ss to 3rd of 5 ch at beg of
round: 8 ch sps.

Round 2: Ss into first ch sp, 3 ch (does NOT count as
st), cluster 3 into same first ch sp, [5 ch, skip 1 dc,
cluster 4 into next ch sp] 7 times, 5 ch, ss to top of
cluster 3 at beg of round.

Break off center color and join in A.

Round 3: 1 ch (does NOT count as st), 1 sc into
same place as ss at end of previous round, [2 ch, 1 dc
into next skipped dc of round 1 enclosing ch loop of
round 2 in st, 2 ch, 1 sc into next cluster 4] 7 times, 2
ch, 1 dc into next skipped dc of round 1 enclosing ch
loop of round 2 in st, 2 ch, ss to first sc: 16 ch sps.

Round 4: Ss into first ch sp, 1 ch (does NOT count as
st), 1 sc into same first ch sp, [3 ch, 1 sc into next ch
sp] 15 times, 3 ch, ss to first sc.

Round 5: Ss into first ch sp, 1 ch (does NOT count as
st), 1 sc into same first ch sp, *3 ch, 1 sc into next ch
sp, 3 ch, (cluster 4, 3 ch and cluster 4) into next ch
sp, [3 ch, 1 sc into next ch sp] twice; rep from * to

end, replacing sc at end of last rep with ss to first sc.
Fasten off.

Motif forms a square. In each corner there is a 3-ch sp between 2 clusters, and along each side there are a further four 3-ch sps. Join motifs while working round 5 by replacing each (3 ch) with (1 ch, 1 sc into corresponding ch sp of adjacent motif, 1 ch).

Bedspread

For single bedspread, make 651 (961) motifs to form one large rectangle 21 (31) motifs wide and 31 motifs long. For double bedspread, make 961 motifs to form one large square 31 motifs wide and 31 motifs long.

Follow the diagram, beginning at the center of the bedspread. Start by making motif 1 using B for rounds 1 and 2 at center. Now make a diamond-shaped band of motif 2, using C for center of motifs. Next make a diamond band of motif 3 using D for centers, then a band of motif 4 using E for centers.

Continue in this way, adding diamond bands of motifs around those already worked, using B for center of next band, C for foll band, D for next band and E for foll band, and so on.
When diamond shape is 21 (31) motifs wide, continue to add motifs as before to end and corner sections, then corner sections only, to create one big rectangle 21 (31) motifs wide and 31 motifs long.

Edging

With RS facing, rejoin A with a ss into a ch sp around outer edge, 1 ch (does NOT count as st, 1 sc into same ch sp, now work around entire outer edge as follows: *3 ch, 1 sc into next ch sp; rep from * to end, replacing sc at end of last rep with ss to first sc: 620 (740) ch sps.

Next round (RS): Ss into first ch sp, 1 ch (does NOT count as st), 3 sc into each ch sp to end, working 3 sc into each corner sc and ending with ss to first sc. Now work 1 round of crab st (sc worked from left to right, instead of right to left) around entire outer edge, ending with ss to first sc.
Fasten off.

					1					
				1	4	1				
			1	4	3	4	1			
		1	4	3	2	3	4	1		
	1	4	3	2	1	2	3	4	1	
		1	4	3	2	3	4	1		
			1	4	3	4	1			
				1	4	1				
					1					

Denim Cushion

The raised textures and the yarn used in Luise Robert's design will ensure that this cushion will improve with age. The denim yarn shrinks when washed, so the cover is made much bigger than required to allow for this—see page 117 for further information.

Materials

Yarn
Denim by Rowan, 1¾oz/50g ball, each approx
   101 yd/93 m (100% cotton)
10 balls in Nashville 225

Hooks and extras
3.00 mm crochet hook
Tapestry needle
25 × ¼ in. (5 mm) glass beads in red
1 × 16 in. (40 cm) zipper in red

Gauge
The gauge used is firm to ensure a tight fabric.
Unwashed: 21 sts and 10 rows to 4 in. (10 cm)
   over a double pattern, using 3.00 mm hook.
   Change hook size, if necessary, to obtain this
   tension.

Special Abbreviations
sctbl = single crochet through the back loop only
sctfl = single crochet through the front loop only
mb = make bobble, work 3dc into the next st
   leaving the last loop on the hook, yo and draw it
   through all the loops on the hook
quintr = quintuple treble. Beaded quintuple treble
   has a bead placed tight against hook, after the
   yarn has been drawn through third pair of loops.
   The st is then completed as usual. Also called trtr,
   or triple treble, due to its ch-6 turning chain.
sp = spike, insert the hook in the base of the
   corresponding st 2 rows back, yo, draw the loop
   up to the height of the adjoining sts, yo, and
   draw the loop through all the loops on the hook
dctbl = double through the next back st loop
dctfl = double through the next front st loop

Sizes and Measurements
To fit: pillow form 16 × 16 in. (40 × 40 cm)
Actual measurements: 15 × 15 in. (38 × 38 cm)

Back Left Section
Ch 40.

Bobble vs. Popcorn
A bobble is a cluster of stitches worked in the same place and joined together at the top—unlike those in a popcorn, which are separate stitches folded around and closed.

Downsizing

The denim yarn shrinks by up to twenty percent in length when washed. As the percentage can vary, the front and back left sections have some additional rows that may be worked and then removed after washing to ensure the correct measurements. The back right section should not require extra rows because the pin tucks restrict the shrinkage to a minimum. If substituting the yarn with a yarn that does not shrink, work the back left section to a measurement of 15 in. (38 cm) and work the front to * before working from row 43 onwards to a length of 15 in. (38 cm).

Row 1 (WS): Skip 3 ch (count as 1 dc), 1 dc into each ch to end, turn: 38 sts.

Row 2: 2 ch (count as 1 sc), 1 sc into each st to end, turn.

Row 3 (WS): 2 ch (count as 1 sc), 1 sc into next st, mb, [2 sc, mb] to last 2 sts, 2 sc, turn.

Row 4: As row 2.

Row 5: 3 ch (count as 1 dc), 1 dc into each st to end, turn.

Rows 6 and 7: As row 5.

Rep rows 2 to 7 seven times, then work rows 2 to 5 again.

Fasten off.

The following rows may be worked to allow for the yarn shrinkage and, if necessary, pulled out after washing:

Work rows 6 and 7, then rows 2 to 5.

Back Right Section

Ch 79.

Row 1 (WS): Skip 3 ch (count as 1 dc), 1 dc into each ch to end, turn: 77 sts.

Row 2: 2 ch (count as 1 sc), 1 sc into each st to end, turn.

Row 3 (base of pin tuck): 3 ch (count as 1 dc), 1 dctbl into each st to end, turn.

Row 4: 3 ch (count as 1 dc), 1 dc into each st to end, turn.

Row 5 (end of pin tuck): Each time picking up front loop left free 2 rows below, work 1 dc into each st to end, turn.

Row 6: 2 ch (count as 1 sc), 1 sc into each st to end, turn.

Row 7: As row 6.

Row 8: 3 ch (count as 1 dc), 1 dc into each st to end, turn.

Row 9: As row 8.

Row 10: As row 6.

Rows 11 and 12: As rows 9 and 10.

Rows 13 to 18: As rows 3 to 8.

Rows 19 and 20: As row 6.

Rep rows 3 to 18, then work row 18 again.

Fasten off.

Front

Ch 79.

Row 1 (WS): Skip 3 ch (count as 1 dc), 1 dc into each ch to end, turn: 77 sts.

Row 2: 2 ch (count as 1 sc), 1 sc into each st to end, turn.

Rows 3 and 4: As row 2.

Row 5: 3 ch (count as 1 dc), 1 dc into each st to end, turn.

Rows 6 and 7: As row 5.

Row 8: 2 ch (count as 1 sc), 1 sctbl into each st to end, turn.

Row 9: 2 ch (count as 1 sc), 1 sctfl into each st to end, turn.

Rows 10 and 11: As rows 8 and 9.

Row 12: As row 8.

Row 13: 3 ch (count as 1 dc), 1 dctfl into each st to end, turn.

Rep rows 2 to 13 twice more.*

Rep rows 2 to 7 again.

Row 44: 2 ch (count as 1 sc), 1 sc into next st, 1 long sc, [2 sc, 1 long sc] to last 2 sts, 2 sc, turn.

Row 45: 2 ch (count as 1 sc), sc into next st, mb, [2 sc, mb] to last 2 sts, 2sc, turn.

Row 46: 2 ch (count as 1 sc), 1 sc into each st to end, turn.

Row 47: As row 46.

Row 48 (base of pin tuck): 3 ch (count as 1 dc), 1 dctfl into each st to end, turn.

Row 49: 3 ch (count as 1 dc), 1 dc into each st to end, turn.

Row 50 (end of pin tuck): *Sc into st and corresponding back loop 2 rows below; rep from * into each st to end, turn.

Rows 51 to 53: As row 46.

Rep the last row twice more.

Rows 54 to 57: As rows 48 to 51.

Rows 58 to 60: As rows 48 to 50.

Row 61: 6 ch (count as 1 quintr), 1 quintr into next st, 1 beaded quintr, [2 quintr, beaded quintr] to last 2 sts, 2 quintr, turn.

Rows 62 and 63: As row 46.

Rows 64 to 67: As rows 48 to 51.

Rows 68 to 77: As rows 48 to 57.

Row 78: As row 46.

Row 79: As row 45.

Rows 80 and 81: As row 5.

Row 82: As row 44.

Row 83: As row 5.

Rows 84 to 86: As row 46.

Fasten off.

The following rows may be worked to allow for the yarn shrinkage and, if necessary, pulled out after washing:

Row 87: 3 ch (count as 1 dc), 1 dc into each st to end, turn.

Row 88: 2 ch (count as 1 sc), 1 sctbl into each st to end, turn.

Row 89: 2 ch (count as 1 sc), 1 sctfl into each st to end, turn.

Rows 90 and 91: As rows 88 and 89.

Row 92: 3 ch (count as 1 dc), 1 dctbl into each st to end, turn.

Row 93: 3 ch (count as 1 dc), 1 dctfl into each st to end, turn.

Finishing

Weave in the ends and launder the worked pieces and the tension swatch at 70°F (21°C) without anything else in the washing machine. Some dye will leach out of the yarn. Unpick any unwanted rows from the back left section and the front and the tension swatch to use for sewing up.

Attach the zipper to the right edge of the back left section and the base chain of the back right section, leaving a ¼ in. (6 mm) gap between the edge of the zipper teeth and the edge of the worked piece. Using slip stitch, sew the back pieces to the front so that the base chain of the back left section aligns with the base chain of the front.

Pillow Talk

For a coordinating cushion, use the remaining yarn to create a 12 in. (30 cm) strip of crochet that can be attached to a 12 in. (30 cm) denim cushion cover. Working on a base chain of 65 sts, work rows 46–78 omitting any beads.

Easy Urban Carryall

Transform an old sheet or unused piece of fabric into a fabulous and unusual bag designed by Sophie Britten—so quick and easy! You can either use colored fabric, or dye the fabric before you start. This is a really easy project and gauge doesn't matter, as the bag can be any size you like, and as you work with a large hook, your bag grows really quickly.

Materials

Yarn
Sheet or old piece of fabric 59 × 78 in.
(150 × 200 cm)

Hook and extras
15 mm crochet hook

Gauge
Gauge is not important for this pattern.

Sizes and Measurements
Actual size: length approx 14 in. (35 cm)

Bag
Tear the sheet lengthways if you can, making strips around 1 in. (2.5 cm) wide. When you have completely shredded the sheet, tie ends of strips together so that you have one continuous length and wind into a ball. It doesn't matter if the strips are uneven, torn-looking or messy—this will barely show in the finished bag and only adds to the vintage look.

Ch 4, join into a ring with ss.

Round 1: Work 7 sc into ring.

Round 2: Work 2 sc into each sc: 14 sts.

Round 3: [1 sc in next sc, 2 sc into next sc] 7 times: 21 sts.

Round 4: 1 sc into each sc to end of round.

Round 5: [1 sc into each of next 2 sc, 2 sc into next sc] 7 times: 28 sts.

Round 6: 1 sc into each sc to end of round.

Round 7: [1 sc into each of next 3 sc, 2 sc into next sc] 7 times: 35 sts.

Rounds 8 and 9: 1 sc into each sc to end of round.

Round 10: [1 sc into next 3 sc, sc2tog] 7 times: 28 sts.

Round 11: 1 sc into each sc to end of round.

Round 12: [1 sc into next 2 sc, sc2tog] 7 times: 21 sts.

Rounds 13–17: 1 sc into each sc to end of round. At the end of round 17 join with ss to first stitch in round.
Fasten off.

Finishing
Tie a length of remaining yarn onto either side of the opening to create a strap. Tuck or weave in any ends.

Babies & Children

Pint-sized projects for the wee set are sure to wrangle plenty of giggles. From the classic Heirloom Teddy Bear to a Hat, Mittens & Booties set for Baby, this chapter brims with something for every little one.

Heirloom Teddy Bear

*Sue Whiting's classic, jointed teddy bear is simply made in rounds of
single crochet in a soft yarn with a sparkle. And, as it is worked in rounds,
it means there is virtually no seaming to do afterwards!*

Materials

Yarn
RYC Soft Lux by Rowan, 1¾oz/50g ball, each
  approx 137 yd/125 m (64% extra fine merino
  wool, 10% angora, 24% nylon, 2% metallic
  fiber)
3 balls in Cashmere 003

Hooks and extras
E/4 (3.50 mm) crochet hook
4 safety-locking toy joints
Pair of safety-locking toy eyes
Brown embroidery floss
40 in. (100 cm) of 1½ in. (4 cm) wide organza
  ribbon
Washable toy fiberfill

Gauge
19 sts and 22 rows to 4 in. (10 cm) measured over
  single crochet fabric using E/4 (3.50 mm) hook.
  Change hook size, if necessary, to obtain this
  gauge.

Sizes and Measurements
Actual measurements: finished height approx
15¾ in. (40 cm)

Arms (Make 2)
Ch 3.

Round 1 (RS): 2 sc into 2nd ch from hook, 4 sc into
last ch, working back along other side of foundation
ch, work 2 sc into same ch as used for first 2 sc, ss to
first sc, turn: 8 sts.

Round 2: 1 ch (does NOT count as st), 2 sc into first
sc, 1 sc into each of next 2 sc, 2 sc into each of next
2 sc, 1 sc into each of next 2 sc, 2 sc into last sc, ss
to first sc, turn: 12 sts.

Round 3: 1 ch (does NOT count as st), 2 sc into first
sc, 1 sc into each of next 4 sc, 2 sc into each of next
2 sc, 1 sc into each of next 4 sc, 2 sc into last sc, ss
to first sc, turn: 16 sts.

Round 4: 1 ch (does NOT count as st), 2 sc into first
sc, 1 sc into each of next 6 sc, 2 sc into each of next
2 sc, 1 sc into each of next 6 sc, 2 sc into last sc, ss
to first sc, turn: 20 sts.

Round 5: 1 ch (does NOT count as st), 2 sc into first
sc, 1 sc into each of next 18 sc, 2 sc into last sc, ss to
first sc, turn: 22 sts.

Round 6: 1 ch (does NOT count as st), 2 sc into first sc, 1 sc into each of next 20 sc, 2 sc into last sc, ss to first sc, turn: 24 sts.

Round 7: 1 ch (does NOT count as st), 1 sc into each sc to end, ss to first sc, turn.

Round 8: 1 ch (does NOT count as st), 2 sc into first sc, 1 sc into each of next 22 sc, 2 sc into last sc, ss to first sc, turn: 26 sts.

Round 9: 1 ch (does NOT count as st), 1 sc into each of first 11 sc, [sc2tog over next 2 sc] twice, 1 sc into each of last 11 sc, ss to first sc, turn: 24 sts.

Round 10: 1 ch (does NOT count as st), 2 sc into first sc, 1 sc into each of next 9 sc, [sc2tog over next 2 sc] twice, 1 sc into each of next 9 sc, 2 sc into last sc, ss to first sc, turn.

Round 11: 1 ch (does NOT count as st), 1 sc into each of first 10 sc, [sc2tog over next 2 sc] twice, 1 sc into each of last 10 sc, ss to first sc, turn: 22 sts.

Round 12: 1 ch (does NOT count as st), 1 sc into each of first 9 sc, [sc2tog over next 2 sc] twice, 1 sc into each of last 9 sc, ss to first sc, turn: 20 sts.

Round 13: 1 ch (does NOT count as st), 2 sc into first sc, 1 sc into each of next 18 sc, 2 sc into last sc, ss to first sc, turn: 22 sts.

Round 14: As round 12: 20 sts.

Round 15: As round 7.

Round 16: 1 ch (does NOT count as st), 2 sc into first sc, 1 sc into each of next 7 sc, [sc2tog over next 2 sc] twice, 1 sc into each of next 7 sc, 2 sc into last sc, ss to first sc, turn.

Rounds 17 to 19: As round 7.

Round 20: 1 ch (does NOT count as st), 2 sc into first sc, 1 sc into each of next 8 sc, 2 sc into each of next 2 sc, 1 sc into each of next 8 sc, 2 sc into last sc, ss to first sc, turn: 24 sts.

Rounds 21 to 28: As round 7.

Left Arm only:
Round 29: As round 7, placing marker after 18th sc.

Right Arm only:
Round 29: As round 7, placing marker after 6th sc.

Both Arms:
Rounds 30 and 31: As round 7.

Round 32: 1 ch (does NOT count as st), sc2tog over first 2 sc, 1 sc into each of next 8 sc, [sc2tog over next 2 sc] twice, 1 sc into each of next 8 sc, sc2tog over last 2 sc, ss to first sc, turn: 20 sts.

Round 33: As round 7.

Round 34: 1 ch (does NOT count as st), sc2tog over first 2 sc, 1 sc into each of next 6 sc, [sc2tog over next 2 sc] twice, 1 sc into each of next 6 sc, sc2tog over last 2 sc, ss to first sc, turn: 16 sts.
Push first half of toy joint through arm at marker, then insert toy fiberfill so Arm is firmly filled.

Round 35: 1 ch (does NOT count as st), sc2tog over first 2 sc, 1 sc into each of next 4 sc, [sc2tog over next 2 sc] twice, 1 sc into each of next 4 sc, sc2tog over last 2 sc, ss to first sc, turn: 12 sts.

Round 36: 1 ch (does NOT count as st), [sc2tog over next 2 sc] 6 times, ss to first sc, turn: 6 sts.
Insert a little more toy fiberfill if required.

Round 37: 1 ch (does NOT count as st), [sc2tog over next 2 sc] 3 times, ss to first sc.
Fasten off.

Legs (Make 2)
Ch 5.

Row 1 (RS): 1 sc into 2nd ch from hook, 1 sc into each of next 3 ch, turn: 4 sts.

Row 2: 1 ch (does NOT count as st), 2 sc into first sc, 1 sc into each of next 2 sc, 2 sc into last sc, turn: 6 sts.

Row 3: 1 ch (does NOT count as st), 1 sc into each sc to end, turn.

Row 4: 1 ch (does NOT count as st), 2 sc into first sc, 1 sc into each of next 4 sc, 2 sc into last sc, turn: 8 sts.

Rows 5 to 10: As row 3.

Row 11: 1 ch (does NOT count as st), sc2tog over first 2 sc, 1 sc into each of next 4 sc, sc2tog over last

2 sc, turn: 6 sts.

Row 12: As row 3.

Row 13: 1 ch (does NOT count as st), sc2tog over first 2 sc, 1 sc into each of next 2 sc, sc2tog over last 2 sc, turn: 4 sts.

Row 14: 1 ch (does NOT count as st), [sc2tog over next 2 sc] twice, turn: 2 sts.

These 14 rows complete paw.

Shape leg, now working in rounds, not rows:

Round 1 (RS): 1 ch (does NOT count as st), skip first sc, 1 sc into next sc, 1 sc into each row-end edge down first side of Paw, 1 sc into each foundation ch, 1 sc into each row-end edge up second side, then 1 sc into sc skipped at beg of round, ss to first sc, turn: 34 sts.

Round 2: 1 ch (does NOT count as st), 1 sc into each sc to end, ss to first sc, turn.

Round 3: 1 ch (does NOT count as st), 1 sc into each of first 15 sc, [sc2tog over next 2 sc] twice, 1 sc into each of last 15 sc, ss to first sc, turn: 32 sts.

Round 4: As round 2.

Round 5: 1 ch (does NOT count as st), 1 sc into each of first 14 sc, [sc2tog over next 2 sc] twice, 1 sc into each of last 14 sc, ss to first sc, turn: 30 sts.

Round 6: 1 ch (does NOT count as st), 1 sc into each of first 13 sc, [sc2tog over next 2 sc] twice, 1 sc into each of last 13 sc, ss to first sc, turn: 28 sts.

Round 7: 1 ch (does NOT count as st), 1 sc into each of first 12 sc, [sc2tog over next 2 sc] twice, 1 sc into each of last 12 sc, ss to first sc, turn: 26 sts.

Round 8: 1 ch (does NOT count as st), 1 sc into each of first 11 sc, [sc2tog over next 2 sc] twice, 1 sc into each of last 11 sc, ss to first sc, turn: 24 sts.

Round 9: 1 ch (does NOT count as st), 1 sc into each of first 10 sc, [sc2tog over next 2 sc] twice, 1 sc into each of last 10 sc, ss to first sc, turn: 22 sts.

Round 10: 1 ch (does NOT count as st), 1 sc into each of first 9 sc, [sc2tog over next 2 sc] twice, 1 sc into each of last 9 sc, ss to first sc, turn: 20 sts.

Round 11: 1 ch (does NOT count as st), 1 sc into each of first 8 sc, [sc2tog over next 2 sc] twice, 1 sc into each of last 8 sc, ss to first sc, turn: 18 sts.

Rounds 12 and 13: As round 2.

Round 14: 1 ch (does NOT count as st), 1 sc into each of first 8 sc, 2 sc into each of next 2 sc, 1 sc into each of last 8 sc, ss to first sc, turn: 20 sts.

Round 15: As round 2.

Round 16: 1 ch (does NOT count as st), 1 sc into each of first 9 sc, 2 sc into each of next 2 sc, 1 sc into each of last 9 sc, ss to first sc, turn: 22 sts.

Round 17: As round 2.

Round 18: 1 ch (does NOT count as st), 1 sc into each of first 10 sc, 2 sc into each of next 2 sc, 1 sc into each of last 10 sc, ss to first sc, turn: 24 sts.

Rounds 19 to 23: As round 2.

Left Leg only:

Round 24: As round 2, placing marker after 6th sc.

Right Leg only:

Round 24: As round 2, placing marker after 18th sc.

Both Legs:

Rounds 25 and 26: As round 2.

Round 27: 1 ch (does NOT count as st), sc2tog over first 2 sc, 1 sc into each of next 8 sc, [sc2tog over next 2 sc] twice, 1 sc into each of next 8 sc, sc2tog over last 2 sc, ss to first sc, turn: 20 sts.

Round 28: 1 ch (does NOT count as st), sc2tog over first 2 sc, 1 sc into each of next 6 sc, [sc2tog over next 2 sc] twice, 1 sc into each of next 6 sc, sc2tog over last 2 sc, ss to first sc, turn: 16 sts.

Push first half of toy joint through leg at marker, then insert toy fiberfill so Leg is firmly filled.

Round 29: 1 ch (does NOT count as st), sc2tog over first 2 sc, 1 sc into each of next 4 sc, [sc2tog over next 2 sc] twice, 1 sc into each of next 4 sc, sc2tog over last 2 sc, ss to first sc, turn: 12 sts.

Round 30: 1 ch (does NOT count as st), [sc2tog over

next 2 sc] 6 times, ss to first sc, turn: 6 sts.
Insert a little more toy fiberfill if required.

Round 31: 1 ch (does NOT count as st), [sc2tog over next 2 sc] 3 times, ss to first sc.
Fasten off.

Body

Ch 2.

Foundation round (WS): 6 sc into 2nd ch from hook, ss to first sc, turn: 6 sts.

Round 1: 1 ch (does NOT count as st), 2 sc into each sc to end, ss to first sc, turn: 12 sts.

Round 2: 1 ch (does NOT count as st), 2 sc into each of first 3 sc, 1 sc into next sc, 2 sc into each of next 4 sc, 1 sc into next sc, 2 sc into each of last 3 sc, ss to first sc, turn: 22 sts.

Round 3: 1 ch (does NOT count as st), 2 sc into first sc, 1 sc into each of next 9 sc, 2 sc into each of next 2 sc, 1 sc into each of next 9 sc, 2 sc into last sc, ss to first sc, turn: 26 sts.

Round 4: 1 ch (does NOT count as st), 2 sc into first sc, 1 sc into each of next 11 sc, 2 sc into each of next 2 sc, 1 sc into each of next 11 sc, 2 sc into last sc, ss to first sc, turn: 30 sts.

Round 5: 1 ch (does NOT count as st), 2 sc into first sc, 1 sc into each of next 13 sc, 2 sc into each of next 2 sc, 1 sc into each of next 13 sc, 2 sc into last sc, ss to first sc, turn: 34 sts.

Round 6: 1 ch (does NOT count as st), 2 sc into first sc, 1 sc into each of next 32 sc, 2 sc into last sc, ss to first sc, turn: 36 sts.

Round 7: 1 ch (does NOT count as st), 1 sc into each of first 17 sc placing marker after 9th of these sc, 2 sc into each of next 2 sc, 1 sc into each of last 17 sc placing marker after 8th of these sc, ss to first sc, turn: 38 sts.

Round 8: 1 ch (does NOT count as st), 2 sc into first sc, 1 sc into each of next 36 sc, 2 sc into last sc, ss to first sc, turn: 40 sts.

Round 9: 1 ch (does NOT count as st), 1 sc into each of first 19 sc, 2 sc into each of next 2 sc, 1 sc into each of last 19 sc, ss to first sc, turn: 42 sts.

Round 10: 1 ch (does NOT count as st), 2 sc into first sc, 1 sc into each of next 40 sc, 2 sc into last sc, ss to first sc, turn: 44 sts.

Round 11: 1 ch (does NOT count as st), 1 sc into each of sc to end, ss to first sc, turn.

Rounds 12 to 17: As round 11.

Round 18: 1 ch (does NOT count as st), 1 sc into each of first 20 sc, [sc2tog over next 2 sc] twice, 1 sc into each of last 20 sc, ss to first sc, turn: 42 sts.

Rounds 19 to 21: As round 11.

Round 22: 1 ch (does NOT count as st), 1 sc into each of first 19 sc, [sc2tog over next 2 sc] twice, 1 sc into each of last 19 sc, ss to first sc, turn: 40 sts.

Round 23: As round 11.

Round 24: 1 ch (does NOT count as st), sc2tog over first 2 sc, 1 sc into each of next 36 sc, sc2tog over last 2 sc, ss to first sc, turn: 38 sts.

Round 25: 1 ch (does NOT count as st), 1 sc into each of first 17 sc, [sc2tog over next 2 sc] twice, 1 sc into each of last 17 sc, ss to first sc, turn: 36 sts.

Rounds 26 and 27: As round 11.

Round 28: 1 ch (does NOT count as st), sc2tog over first 2 sc, 1 sc into each of next 14 sc, [sc2tog over next 2 sc] twice, 1 sc into each of next 14 sc, sc2tog over last 2 sc, ss to first sc, turn: 32 sts.

Round 29: As round 11.

Round 30: 1 ch (does NOT count as st), 1 sc into each of first 14 sc, [sc2tog over next 2 sc] twice, 1 sc into each of last 14 sc, ss to first sc, turn: 30 sts.

Round 31: As round 11.

Round 32: 1 ch (does NOT count as st), sc2tog over first 2 sc, 1 sc into each of next 11 sc placing marker after 5th of these sc, [sc2tog over next 2 sc] twice, 1 sc into each of next 11 sc placing marker after 6th of these sc, sc2tog over last 2 sc, ss to first sc, turn: 26 sts.

Round 33: As round 11.

Round 34: 1 ch (does NOT count as st), 1 sc into each of first 11 sc, [sc2tog over next 2 sc] twice, 1 sc into each of last 11 sc, ss to first sc, turn: 24 sts.

Round 35: 1 ch (does NOT count as st), sc2tog over first 2 sc, 1 sc into each of next 8 sc, [sc2tog over next 2 sc] twice, 1 sc into each of next 8 sc, sc2tog over last 2 sc, ss to first sc, turn: 20 sts.

Push Leg joints through Body at marked points of round 7, ensuring paws point forwards (start and end of Body rounds is center back) and secure joints by attaching backing disks. In same way, attach Arms to marked points of round 32. Insert toy fiberfill so Body is firmly filled.

Round 36: 1 ch (does NOT count as st), 1 sc into each of first 8 sc, [sc2tog over next 2 sc] twice, 1 sc into each of last 8 sc, ss to first sc, turn: 18 sts.

Round 37: 1 ch (does NOT count as st), sc2tog over first 2 sc, 1 sc into each of next 5 sc, [sc2tog over next 2 sc] twice, 1 sc into each of next 5 sc, sc2tog over last 2 sc, ss to first sc, turn: 14 sts.

Round 38: 1 ch (does NOT count as st), sc2tog over first 2 sc, 1 sc into each of next 3 sc, [sc2tog over next 2 sc] twice, 1 sc into each of next 3 sc, sc2tog over last 2 sc, ss to first sc, turn: 10 sts.
Fasten off.

Head

Ch 20 and join with a ss to form a ring.

Round 1 (RS): 1 ch (does NOT count as st), 2 sc into each ch to end, ss to first sc, turn: 40 sts.

Round 2: 1 ch (does NOT count as st), 2 sc into first sc, 1 sc into each of next 6 sc, 2 sc into each of next 2 sc, 1 sc into each of next 10 sc, 2 sc into each of next 2 sc, 1 sc into each of next 10 sc, 2 sc into each of next 2 sc, 1 sc into each of next 6 sc, 2 sc into last sc, ss to first sc, turn: 48 sts.

Round 3: 1 ch (does NOT count as st), 1 sc into each of first 9 sc, 2 sc into next sc, 1 sc into each of next 13 sc, 2 sc into each of next 2 sc, 1 sc into each of next 13 sc, 2 sc into next sc, 1 sc into each of last 9 sc, ss to first sc, turn: 52 sts.

Round 4: 1 ch (does NOT count as st), 2 sc into first sc, 1 sc into each of next 24 sc, 2 sc into each of next 2 sc, 1 sc into each of next 24 sc, 2 sc into last sc, ss to first sc, turn: 56 sts.

Round 5: 1 ch (does NOT count as st), 1 sc into each of first 12 sc, 2 sc into next sc, 1 sc into each of next 14 sc, 2 sc into each of next 2 sc, 1 sc into each of next 14 sc, 2 sc into next sc, 1 sc into each of last 12 sc, ss to first sc, turn: 60 sts.

Round 6: 1 ch (does NOT count as st), 1 sc into each of first 11 sc, 2 sc into next sc, 1 sc into each of next 16 sc, 2 sc into each of next 4 sc, 1 sc into each of next 16 sc, 2 sc into next sc, 1 sc into each of last 11 sc, ss to first sc, turn: 66 sts.

Round 7: 1 ch (does NOT count as st), 1 sc into each of first 32 sc, 2 sc into each of next 2 sc, 1 sc into each of last 32 sc, ss to first sc, turn: 68 sts.

Round 8: 1 ch (does NOT count as st), 1 sc into each of first 33 sc, 2 sc into each of next 2 sc, 1 sc into each of last 33 sc, ss to first sc, turn: 70 sts.

Round 9: 1 ch (does NOT count as st), 2 sc into first sc, 1 sc into each of next 33 sc, 2 sc into each of next 2 sc, 1 sc into each of next 33 sc, 2 sc into last sc, turn: 74 sts.

Round 10: 1 ch (does NOT count as st), 1 sc into each of first 36 sc, 2 sc into each of next 2 sc, 1 sc into each of last 36 sc, ss to first sc, turn: 76 sts.

Round 11: 1 ch (does NOT count as st), 1 sc into each of first 37 sc, 2 sc into each of next 2 sc, 1 sc into each of last 37 sc, ss to first sc, turn: 78 sts.

Round 12: 1 ch (does NOT count as st), 1 sc into each of first 12 sc, [sc2tog over next 2 sc] twice placing marker between these 2 sts to denote base of ear, 1 sc into each of next 46 sc, [sc2tog over next 2 sc] twice placing marker between these 2 sts to denote base of ear, 1 sc into each of last 12 sc, ss to first sc, turn: 74 sts.

Round 13: 1 ch (does NOT count as st), 1 sc into each sc to end, ss to first sc, turn.

Round 14: 1 ch (does NOT count as st), 1 sc into each of first 12 sc, 2 sc into each of next 2 sc, 1 sc into each of next 46 sc, 2 sc into each of next 2 sc, 1 sc into each of last 12 sc, ss to first sc, turn: 78 sts.

Round 15: 1 ch (does NOT count as st), 1 sc into each of first 13 sc, 2 sc into each of next 2 sc, 1 sc into each of next 48 sc, 2 sc into each of next 2 sc, 1 sc into each of last 13 sc, ss to first sc, turn: 82 sts.

Round 16: As round 13.

Round 17: 1 ch (does NOT count as st), 1 sc into each of first 14 sc, 2 sc into each of next 2 sc, 1 sc into each of next 21 sc, [sc2tog over next 2 sc] 4 times, 1 sc into each of next 21 sc, 2 sc into each of next 2 sc, 1 sc into each of last 14 sc, ss to first sc, turn: 82 sts.

Round 18: 1 ch (does NOT count as st), 1 sc into each of first 37 sc, [sc2tog over next 2 sc] 4 times, 1 sc into each of last 37 sc, ss to first sc, turn: 78 sts.

Round 19: 1 ch (does NOT count as st), sc2tog over first 2 sc, 1 sc into each of next 33 sc, [sc2tog over next 2 sc] 4 times, 1 sc into each of next 33 sc, sc2tog over last 2 sc, ss to first sc, turn: 72 sts.

Round 20: 1 ch (does NOT count as st), 1 sc into each of first 34 sc, [sc2tog over next 2 sc] twice, 1 sc into each of last 34 sc, ss to first sc, turn: 70 sts.

Round 21: 1 ch (does NOT count as st), 1 sc into each of first 33 sc, [sc2tog over next 2 sc] twice, 1 sc into each of last 33 sc, ss to first sc, turn: 68 sts.

Round 22: 1 ch (does NOT count as st), 1 sc into each of first 32 sc, [sc2tog over next 2 sc] twice, 1 sc into each of last 32 sc, ss to first sc, turn: 66 sts.

Round 23: 1 ch (does NOT count as st), sc2tog over first 2 sc, 1 sc into each of next 11 sc, [sc2tog over next 2 sc] twice, 1 sc into each of next 32 sc, [sc2tog over next 2 sc] twice, 1 sc into each of next 11 sc, sc2tog over last 2 sc, ss to first sc, turn: 60 sts.

Round 24: 1 ch (does NOT count as st), 1 sc into each of first 28 sc, [sc2tog over next 2 sc] twice, 1 sc into each of last 28 sc, ss to first sc, turn: 58 sts.

Shape first top of ear.
Remove hook from working loop but do NOT fasten off. With RS facing, skip first 6 sc of next round, rejoin new length of yarn to next st.

Next round (RS): **1 ch (does NOT count as st), 1 sc into sc where yarn is rejoined, 1 sc into each of next 4 sc, [sc2tog over next 2 sc] twice, 1 sc into each of next 5 sc, ss to first sc of this round, turn: 12 sts.

Next round: 1 ch (does NOT count as st), sc2tog over first 2 sc, 1 sc into each of next 2 sc, [sc2tog over next 2 sc] twice, 1 sc into each of next 2 sc, sc2tog over last 2 sc, ss to first sc, turn: 8 sts.
Fold Ear flat with RS together and work one row of sc across top of Ear to join upper edges.
Fasten off.**

Shape second top of ear:

Return to top of round 24. With RS facing, skip next 18 sc after first ear top. Join length of yarn to next st and work as given for first ear top from ** to **.

Complete head:

Return to round 24, slip working loop back onto hook.

Round 25 (RS): 1 ch (does NOT count as st), 1 sc into each of first 13 sc (ear top is between 6th and 7th of these sts), [sc2tog over next 2 sc] twice, 1 sc into each of last 13 sc (ear top is between 7th and 8th of these sts), ss to first sc, turn: 28 sts.

Round 26: 1 ch (does NOT count as st), 1 sc into each of first 4 sc, *[sc2tog over next 2 sc] twice, 1 sc into each of next 4 sc, rep from * twice more, ss to first sc, turn: 22 sts.

Round 27: 1 ch (does NOT count as st), 1 sc into each of first 3 sc, *[sc2tog over next 2 sc] twice, 1 sc into each of next 2 sc, rep from * once more, [sc2tog over next 2 sc] twice, 1 sc into each of last 3 sc, ss to first sc, turn: 16 sts.

Round 28: 1 ch (does NOT count as st), [sc2tog over next 2 sc] 8 times, ss to first sc, turn: 8 sts.

Round 29: 1 ch (does NOT count as st), [sc2tog over next 2 sc] 4 times, ss to first sc: 4 sts.
Fasten off.

Finishing

Run gathering thread around top of last round, pull up tightly to close opening and fasten off securely. Fold ears flat and stitch through both layers from marker on round 12 to ear division of round 25. Insert toy fiberfill so that Head is firmly filled. Using photograph as a guide, attach eyes to Head. Using embroidery floss and photograph as a guide, embroider satin stitch nose, and back stitch mouth. Insert a little more toy fiberfill into neck of both Head and Body, then sew Head to Body. Tie ribbon in a bow around neck.

Striped Sweater

Textures and stripes in bright colors team up to make this jolly design by Sue Whiting for babies and toddlers. A simple combination of trebles and single crochet creates the bobble effect and the yarn is comfortable pure cotton. See page 136 for the cardigan that can be made to match.

Materials

Yarn

Handknit Cotton DK by Rowan, 1¾oz/50g ball, each approx 92 yd/85 m (100% cotton)

3 (3, 4, 4) balls in Chime 204 (A)

3 (3, 4, 4) balls in Bleached 263 (B)

3 (3, 4, 4) balls in Gooseberry 219 (C)

Hooks and extras

E/4 (3.50 mm) crochet hook

1 small button

Gauge

17 sts and 16 rows to 4 in. (10 cm) measured over pattern using E/4 (3.50 mm) hook. Change hook size, if necessary, to obtain this gauge.

Sizes and Measurements

To fit: chest 20 (22, 24, 26) in. [51 (56, 61, 66) cm]

Actual measurements: chest 22¾ (24½, 27, 29) in. [58 (62, 69, 74) cm]; **length** 11¾ (13¼, 15¼, 17) in. [30 (34, 39, 43) cm]; **sleeve** 8¼ (10½, 12¼, 13¾) in. [21 (27, 31, 35) cm]

Back

With A, ch 50 (54, 60, 64).

Foundation row (RS): 1 sc into 2nd ch from hook, 1 sc into each ch to end, turn: 49 (53, 59, 63) sts.

Cont in patt. Join in B.

Row 1: Using B, 1 ch (does NOT count as st), 1 sc into first sc, *1 tr into next sc, 1 sc into next sc; rep from * to end, turn.

Join in C.

Row 2: Using C, 1 ch (does NOT count as st), 1 sc into each sc and tr to end, turn.

Row 3: Using A, 1 ch (does NOT count as st), 1 sc into each of first 2 sc, *1 tr into next sc, 1 sc into next sc; rep from * to last st, 1 sc into last sc, turn.

Row 4: Using B, 1 ch (does NOT count as st), 1 sc into each sc and tr to end, turn.

Row 5: Using C, 1 ch (does NOT count as st), 1 sc into first sc, *1 tr into next sc, 1 sc into next sc; rep from * to end, turn.

Row 6: Using A, 1 ch (does NOT count as st), 1 sc into each sc and tr to end, turn.

Row 7: Using B, 1 ch (does NOT count as st), 1 sc into each of first 2 sc, *1 tr into next sc, 1 sc into next sc; rep from * to last st, 1 sc into last sc, turn.

Row 8: As row 2.

Row 9: Using A, 1 ch (does NOT count as st), 1 sc into first sc, *1 tr into next sc, 1 sc into next sc; rep from * to end, turn.

Row 10: As row 4.

Row 11: Using C, 1 ch (does NOT count as st), 1 sc into each of first 2 sc, *1 tr into next sc, 1 sc into next sc; rep from * to last st, 1 sc into last sc, turn.

Row 12: As row 6.

These 12 rows form patt.

**Cont in patt until Back measures 6¼ (7½, 9, 10¼) in. [16 (19, 23, 26) cm], ending after a WS row.

Shape armholes:

Place markers at both ends of last row to denote base of armholes.

Next row: 1 ch (does NOT count as st), sc2tog over first 2 sts—1 st decreased, patt to last 2 sts, sc2tog over last 2 sts—1 st decreased, turn.

Rep last row 4 (4, 5, 5) times more: 39 (43, 47, 51) sts**.

Cont in patt until armholes measure 2 (2¼, 2¾, 3) in. [5 (6, 7, 8) cm], ending after a WS row.

Divide for back opening:

Next row (RS): 1 ch (does NOT count as st), 1 sc into each of first 19 (21, 23, 25) sts and turn, leaving rem sts unworked.

Work on these sts only for first side.

Cont in patt until armhole measures 4¾ (5, 5½, 6) in. [12 (13, 14, 15) cm], ending after a RS row.

Fasten off.

Return to last complete row worked, skip center st, rejoin appropriate yarn to next st with RS facing, 1 ch (does NOT count as st), 1 sc into st where yarn was rejoined, 1 sc into each st to end, turn: 19 (21, 23, 25) sts.

Complete second side to match first.

Front

Work as for Back to **.

Cont straight until 7 (7, 9, 9) rows less have been worked than on Back to shoulder fasten-off row, ending after a WS row.

Shape front neck:

Next row (RS): 1 ch (does NOT count as st), 1 sc into each of first 15 (16, 18, 19) sts and turn, leaving rem sts unworked.

Work on these sts only for first side of neck.

Dec 1 st at neck edge on next 3 rows, then on foll 1 (1, 2, 2) alt rows: 11 (12, 13, 14) sts.

Work 1 row, ending after a RS row.

Fasten off.

Return to last complete row worked, skip center 9 (11, 11, 13) sts, rejoin appropriate yarn to next st with RS facing, 1 ch (does NOT count as st), 1 sc into st were yarn was rejoined, 1 sc into each st to end, turn: 15 (16, 18, 19) sts.

Complete second side to match first.

Sleeves

With A, ch 28 (30, 32, 34).

Work foundation row as for Back: 27 (29, 31, 33) sts.

Cont in patt as for Back.

Work 1 (3, 3, 3) rows.

Next row (RS): 1 ch (does NOT count as st), 2 sc into first sc—1 st increased, 1 sc into each st to last st, 2 sc into last st—1 st increased, turn.

Working all increases as set by last row, inc 1 st at each end of every foll 4th row until there are 41 (41, 45, 47) sts, taking inc sts into patt.

2nd, 3rd and 4th sizes only:
Inc 1 st at each end of every foll 6th row until there are (45, 49, 53) sts.

All sizes:
Cont straight until Sleeve measures 7½ (9¾, 11½, 13) in. [19 (25, 29, 33) cm], ending after a WS (WS, RS, RS) row.

Shape top:
Place markers at both ends of last row to denote base of armholes.
Dec 1 st at each end of next 5 (5, 6, 6) rows, ending after a RS row: 31 (35, 37, 41) sts.
Fasten off.

Finishing
Join shoulder seams. Matching markers and center of top of last row of sleeves to shoulder seams, sew sleeves into armholes. Sew side and sleeve seams.

Make neck border:
With RS facing, using E/4 (3.50 mm) hook and A, attach yarn at top of left side of back opening and work around neck edge as follows: 1 ch (does NOT count as st), work 1 row of sc evenly around neck edge, ending at top of right side of back opening, turn.
Row 2: 1 ch (does NOT count as st), 1 sc into each sc to end, turn.
Rep last row twice more, ending after a WS row.
Fasten off.

Make back opening border:
With RS facing, using E/4 (3.50 mm) hook and A, attach yarn at beg of last row of neck border and work around back opening edge as follows: 1 ch (does NOT count as st), work 1 row of sc evenly down right side of back opening, then up left side of back opening, ending at end of last row of neck

border, turn, 3 ch (to form button loop), skip last 3 sc of previous row, ss to next sc.
Fasten off.

Make hem edging:
With RS facing, using E/4 (3.50 mm) hook and A, attach yarn at base of one side seam and work around lower edge as follows: 1 ch (does NOT count as st), work 1 round of sc evenly around entire hem edge, ss to first sc, turn.
Round 2: 1 ch (does NOT count as st), 1 sc into each sc to end, ss to first sc, turn.
Rep last round twice more, ending after a WS round.
Fasten off.

Make cuff edging:
Work as for hem edging, rejoining yarn at base of sleeve seam.
Sew on button.

Match Point
The picture on page 133 shows this sweater made in Chime, Bleached and Gooseberry, as specified on page 132, and the matching cardigan is shown on page 137 in Sugar, Lupin and Seafarer as specified in the pattern on page 136. Try making them both in the same colors for a smart, matching set, or make a plain sweater in just one of the colors to go with the cardigan.

Striped Cardigan

This cheerful cardigan designed by Sue Whiting uses textures and stripes to create a spirited design. A simple combination of treble and single crochet creates the bobble effect and the yarn is a comfortable pure cotton. See page 132 for a sweater that can be made to match.

Materials

Yarn

Handknit Cotton DK by Rowan, 1¾oz/50g ball,
   each approx 92 yd/85 m (100% cotton)
3 (4, 4, 5) balls in Sugar 303 (A)
3 (3, 4, 4) balls in Lupin 305 (B)
3 (3, 4, 4) balls in Seafarer 318 (C)

Hooks and extras

E/4 (3.50 mm) crochet hook
5 buttons

Gauge

17 sts and 16 rows to 4 in. (10 cm) measured over
   pattern using E/4 (3.50 mm) hook. Change hook
   size, if necessary, to obtain this gauge.

Sizes and Measurements

To fit: chest 20 (22, 24, 26) in. [51 (56, 61, 66) cm]
Actual measurements: chest 22¾ (24½, 27, 29) in. [58 (62, 69, 74) cm]; **length** 11½ (13, 15, 16½) in. [29 (33, 38, 42) cm]; **sleeve** 7¾ (10¼, 11¾, 13¼) in. [20 (26, 30, 34) cm]

Back

With E/4 (3.50 mm) hook and A, ch 50 (54, 60, 63).
Foundation row (RS): 1 sc into 2nd ch from hook, 1 sc into each ch to end, turn: 49 (53, 59, 63) sts.
Cont in patt. Join in B.
Row 1: Using B, 1 ch (does NOT count as st), 1 sc into first sc, *1 tr into next sc, 1 sc into next sc; rep from * to end, turn.
Join in C.
Row 2: Using C, 1 ch (does NOT count as st), 1 sc into each sc and tr to end, turn.
Row 3: Using A, 1 ch (does NOT count as st), 1 sc into each of first 2 sc, *1 tr into next sc, 1 sc into next sc; rep from * to last st, 1 sc into last sc, turn.
Row 4: Using B, 1 ch (does NOT count as st), 1 sc into each sc and tr to end, turn.
Row 5: Using C, 1 ch (does NOT count as st), 1 sc into first sc, *1 tr into next sc, 1 sc into next sc; rep from * to end, turn.
Row 6: Using A, 1 ch (does NOT count as st), 1 sc into each sc and tr to end, turn.

Row 7: Using B, 1 ch (does NOT count as st), 1 sc into each of first 2 sc, *1 tr into next sc, 1 sc into next sc; rep from * to last st, 1 sc into last sc, turn.

Row 8: As row 2.

Row 9: Using A, 1 ch (does NOT count as st), 1 sc into first sc, *1 tr into next sc, 1 sc into next sc; rep from * to end, turn.

Row 10: As row 4.

Row 11: Using C, 1 ch (does NOT count as st), 1 sc into each of first 2 sc, *1 tr into next sc, 1 sc into next sc; rep from * to last st, 1 sc into last sc, turn.

Row 12: As row 6.

These 12 rows form patt.

Cont in patt until Back measures 6¼ (7½, 9, 10¼) in. [16 (19, 23, 26) cm], ending after a RS row.

Shape armholes:

Place markers at both ends of last row to denote base of armholes.

Next row: 1 ch (does NOT count as st), sc2tog over first 2 sts—1 st decreased, patt to last 2 sts, dc2tog over last 2 sts—1 st decreased, turn.

Rep last row 4 (4, 5, 5) times more: 39 (43, 47, 51) sts.

Cont in patt until armholes measure 4¾ (5, 5½, 6) in. [12 (13, 14, 15) cm], ending after a RS row.

Fasten off.

Left Front

With E/4 (3.50 mm) hook and A, ch 24 (26, 29, 31).

Work foundation row as for Back: 23 (25, 28, 30) sts.

Cont in patt as for Back until Left Front matches Back to start of armhole shaping, ending after a WS row— note for 3rd and 4th sizes only, beg 1st, 5th and 9th rows with 2 sc and 3rd, 7th and 11th rows with 1 sc.

Shape armhole:

Place marker at end of last row to denote base of armhole.

Working all decreases in same way as for Back, dec 1 st at armhole edge of next 5 (5, 6, 6) rows: 18 (20, 22, 24) sts.

Cont straight until 7 (7, 9, 9) rows less have been worked than on Back to shoulder fasten-off row, ending after a WS row.

Shape neck:

Next row (RS): 1 ch (does NOT count as st), 1 sc into each of first 15 (16, 18, 19) sts and turn, leaving rem 3 (4, 4, 5) sts unworked.

Dec 1 st at neck edge on next 3 rows, then on foll 1 (1, 2, 2) alt rows: 11 (12, 13, 14) sts.

Work 1 row, ending after a RS row.

Fasten off.

Right Front

With E/4 (3.50 mm) hook and A, ch 24 (26, 29, 31).

Work foundation row as for Back: 23 (25, 28, 30) sts.

Cont in patt as Back until Right Front matches Back to beg of armhole shaping, ending after WS row— note for 3rd and 4th sizes only, end 1st, 5th and 9th rows with 2 sc and 3rd, 7th and 11th rows with 1 sc.

Shape armhole:

Place marker at beg of last row to denote base of armhole.

Working all decreases as for Back, dec 1 st at armhole edge of next 5 (5, 6, 6) rows: 18 (20, 22, 24) sts.

Cont straight until 7 (7, 9, 9) rows less have been worked than on Back to shoulder fasten-off row, ending after a WS row.

Break yarn.

Shape neck:

Next row (RS): Skip first 3 (4, 4, 5) sts, rejoin appropriate yarn to next st, 1 ch (does NOT count as st), 1 sc into each st to end, turn: 15 (16, 18, 19) sts.

Dec 1 st at neck edge on next 3 rows, then on foll 1
(1, 2, 2) alt rows: 11 (12, 13, 14) sts.
Work 1 row, ending after a RS row.
Fasten off.

Sleeves
With 3.50mm hook and A, ch 28 (30, 32, 34).
Work foundation row as for Back: 27 (29, 31, 33) sts.

Cont in patt as for Back. Work 1 (3, 3, 3) rows.
Next row (RS): 1 ch (does NOT count as st), 2 sc
into first sc—1 st increased, 1 sc into each st to last
st, 2 sc into last st—1 st increased, turn.
Working all increases as set by last row, inc 1 st at
each end of every foll 4th row until there are 41 (41,
45, 47) sts, taking inc sts into patt.

2nd, 3rd and 4th sizes only:
Inc 1 st at each end of every foll 6th row until there
are (45, 49, 53) sts.

All sizes:
Cont straight until Sleeve measures 7½ (9¾, 11½,
13) in. [19 (25, 29, 33) cm], ending after a WS (WS,
RS, RS) row.

Shape top:
Place markers at both ends of last row to denote
base of armholes.
Dec 1 st at each end of next 5 (5, 6, 6) rows, ending
after a RS row: 31 (35, 37, 41) sts.
Fasten off.

Finishing
Join shoulder seams. Matching markers and center of
top of last row of sleeves to shoulder seams, sew
sleeves into armholes. Sew side and sleeve seams.

Make neck, hem and front border:
With RS facing, using E/4 (3.50 mm) hook and A,
attach yarn at base of a side seam and work: 1 ch
(does NOT count as st), 1 round of sc evenly around
hem, front opening and neck edge, with 3 sc into
each corner sc, end with ss to first sc, turn.
Mark positions for 5 buttonholes evenly along right
front opening edge—first 2 in. (5 cm) up from lower
edge, last level with start of neck shaping.
Round 2: 1 ch (does NOT count as st), 1 sc into each
sc to end, making buttonholes to correspond with
positions marked by replacing (1 sc into each of next
2 sc) with (2 ch, skip 2 sc), working 3 sc into each
corner sc and ending with ss to first sc, turn.
Round 3: 1 ch (does NOT count as st), 1 sc into each
sc to end, working 2 sc into each buttonhole ch sp
and 3 sc into each corner sc, and ending with ss to
first sc, turn.
Round 4: 1 ch (does NOT count as st), 1 sc into each
sc to end, working 3 sc into corner sc and ending
with ss to first sc.
Fasten off.

Make cuff edging:
With RS facing, using E/4 (3.50 mm) hook and A,
attach yarn at base of one sleeve seam and work
around cuff edge as follows: 1 ch (does NOT count as
st), work 1 round of sc evenly around entire cuff
edge, ss to first sc, turn.
Round 2: 1 ch (does NOT count as st), 1 sc into each
sc to end, ss to first sc, turn.
Rep last round twice more, ending after a WS round.
Fasten off and sew on buttons.

Baby's Hat, Mittens & Booties

Sue Whiting's oh-so-cute pull-on hat, mittens and booties make the perfect gift for any new mother. Using a soft cashmere blend yarn, they are crocheted using just single crochet fabric with a lacy scallop edging and ribbon trim.

Materials

Yarn
RYC Cashsoft 4 ply by Rowan, 1¾oz/50g ball, each
    approx 197 yd/180 m (57% extra fine merino
    wool, 33% microfiber, 10% cashmere)
2 balls in Roselake 421

Hooks and extras
3.00 mm crochet hook
3 yd (2.70 m) of ¼ in. (6 mm) wide satin ribbon

Gauge
24 sts and 27 rows to 4 in. (10 cm) measured over
    single crochet fabric using 3.00 mm hook. Change
    hook size, if necessary, to obtain this gauge.

Sizes and Measurements
To fit: newborn–3-month-old baby
Actual measurements: hat width around head
14½ in. (37 cm); **mittens width around hand** 4¼
in. (11 cm); **booties length of foot** 4 in. (10 cm).

Hat
Ch 2.
Round 1 (RS): 8 sc into 2nd ch from hook, ss to first sc, turn: 8 sts.
Round 2 (WS): 1 ch (does NOT count as st), 2 sc into each sc to end, ss to first sc, turn: 16 sts.
Round 3: 1 ch (does NOT count as st), [1 sc into next sc, 2 sc into next sc] 8 times, ss to first sc, turn: 24 sts.
Round 4: 1 ch (does NOT count as st), [2 sc into next sc, 1 sc into each of next 2 sc] 8 times, ss to first sc, turn: 32 sts.
Round 5: 1 ch (does NOT count as st), [1 sc into each of next 3 sc, 2 sc into next sc] 8 times, ss to first sc, turn: 40 sts.
Round 6: 1 ch (does NOT count as st), 1 sc into each sc to end, ss to first sc, turn.
Round 7: 1 ch (does NOT count as st), [1 sc into each of next 4 sc, 2 sc into next sc] 8 times, ss to first sc, turn: 48 sts.

Round 8: As round 6.

Round 9: 1 ch (does NOT count as st), [1 sc into each of next 5 sc, 2 sc into next sc] 8 times, ss to first sc, turn: 56 sts.

Round 10: As round 6.

Round 11: 1 ch (does NOT count as st), [1 sc into each of next 6 sc, 2 sc into next sc] 8 times, ss to first sc, turn: 64 sts.

Round 12: As round 6.

Round 13: 1 ch (does NOT count as st), [1 sc into each of next 7 sc, 2 sc into next sc] 8 times, ss to first sc, turn: 72 sts.

Round 14: As round 6.

Round 15: 1 ch (does NOT count as st), [1 sc into each of next 8 sc, 2 sc into next sc] 8 times, ss to first sc, turn: 80 sts.

Round 16: As round 6.

Round 17: 1 ch (does NOT count as st), [1 sc into each of next 9 sc, 2 sc into next sc] 8 times, ss to first sc, turn: 88 sts.

Rounds 18 to 34: As round 6.

Round 35 (RS): 3 ch (counts as first hdc and 1 ch), skip st at base of 3 ch and next sc, *1 hdc into next sc, 1 ch, skip 1 sc; rep from * to end, ss to 2nd of 3 ch at beg of round, do NOT turn: 44 ch sps.

Round 36 (RS): ss into first ch sp, 1 ch (does NOT count as st), (1 sc, 3 ch and 1 dc) into same ch sp, *3 ch, 7 dc into ch sp formed by last dc, skip 1 ch sp**, (1 sc, 3 ch and 1 dc) into next ch sp; rep from * to end, ending last rep at **, ss to first sc: 22 patt reps. Fasten off.

Mittens (Both alike)

Ch 6.

Round 1 (RS): 2 sc into 2nd ch from hook, 1 sc into each of next 3 ch, 4 sc into last ch, working back along other side of foundation ch: 1 sc into each of next 3 ch, 2 sc into last ch (this is same ch as used for first 2 sc), ss to first sc, turn: 14 sts.

Round 2: 1 ch (does NOT count as st), 2 sc into first sc, 1 sc into each of next 5 sc, 2 sc into each of next 2 sc, 1 sc into each of next 5 sc, 2 sc into last sc, ss to first sc, turn: 18 sts.

Round 3: 1 ch (does NOT count as st), 2 sc into first sc, 1 sc into each of next 7 sc, 2 sc into each of next 2 sc, 1 sc into each of next 7 sc, 2 sc into last sc, ss to first sc, turn: 22 sts.

Round 4: 1 ch (does NOT count as st), 1 sc into each sc to end, ss to first sc, turn.

Round 5: 1 ch (does NOT count as st), 2 sc into first sc, 1 sc into each of next 9 sc, 2 sc into each of next 2 sc, 1 sc into each of next 9 sc, 2 sc into last sc, ss to first sc, turn: 26 sts.

Rounds 6 to 19: As round 4.

Round 20: 1 ch (does NOT count as st), sc2tog over first 2 sc, 1 sc into each of next 11 sc, sc2tog over next 2 sc, 1 sc into each of next 11 sc, ss to first sc, turn: 24 sts.

Complete mitten by working rounds 35 and 36 as for hat, noting there will be 12 ch sps after first of these rounds and 6 patt reps after 2nd of these rounds. Fasten off.

Booties (Both alike)

With 3.00 mm hook, ch 17.

Round 1 (RS): 2 sc into 2nd ch from hook, 1 sc into each of next 14 ch, 4 sc into last ch, working back along other side of foundation ch: 1 sc into each of next 14 ch, 2 sc into last ch (this is same ch as used for first 2 sc), ss to first sc, turn: 36 sts.

Round 2: 1 ch (does NOT count as st), 1 sc into first sc, 2 sc into next sc, 1 sc into each of next 14 sc, 2 sc into next sc, 1 sc into each of next 2 sc, 2 sc into next sc, 1 sc into each of next 14 sc, 2 sc into next sc, 1 sc into last sc, ss to first sc, turn: 40 sts.

Round 3: 1 ch (does NOT count as st), 2 sc into first sc, 1 sc into each of next 18 sc, 2 sc into each of next 2 sc, 1 sc into each of next 18 sc, 2 sc into last sc, ss to first sc, turn: 44 sts.

Round 4: 1 ch (does NOT count as st), 1 sc into each

of first 3 sc, 2 sc into next sc, 1 sc into each of next 14 sc, 2 sc into next sc, 1 sc into each of next 6 sc, 2 sc into next sc, 1 sc into each of next 14 sc, 2 sc into next sc, 1 sc into each of last 3 sc, ss to first sc, turn: 48 sts.

Round 5: 1 ch (does NOT count as st), 2 sc into first sc, 1 sc into each of next 3 sc, 2 sc into next sc, 1 sc into each of next 14 sc, 2 sc into next sc, 1 sc into each of next 3 sc, 2 sc into each of next 2 sc, 1 sc into each of next 3 sc, 2 sc into next sc, 1 sc into each of next 14 sc, 2 sc into next sc, 1 sc into each of next 3 sc, 2 sc into last sc, ss to first sc, turn: 56 sts.

Round 6: 1 ch (does NOT count as st), 1 sc into each of first 3 sc, 2 sc into next sc, 1 sc into each of next 20 sc, 2 sc into next sc, 1 sc into each of next 6 sc, 2 sc into next sc, 1 sc into each of next 20 sc, 2 sc into next sc, 1 sc into each of last 3 sc, ss to first sc, turn: 60 sts.

Round 7: 1 ch (does NOT count as st), 1 sc into each of sc to end, ss to first sc, turn.

Rounds 8 to 12: As round 7.

Shape instep:

Row 13: 1 ch (does NOT count as st), 1 sc into each of first 33 sc, sc3tog over next 3 sc, turn.

Row 14: 1 ch (does NOT count as st), 1 sc into each of first 7 sts, sc3tog over next 3 sts, turn.

Row 15: 1 ch (does NOT count as st), 1 sc into each of first 7 sts, sc3tog over next 3 sts—these are last st of Instep and next 2 sts of round 12, turn.

Row 16: 1 ch (does NOT count as st), 1 sc into each of first 7 sts, sc3tog over next 3 sts—these are last st of Instep and next 2 sts of row 13, turn.

Rows 17 to 24: Repeat rows 15 and 16 four times more.

Row 25: 1 ch (does NOT count as st), 1 sc into each of first 8 sts, 1 sc into each of rem 14 sc of round 12, ss to sc at beg of row 13 of instep, turn.

Round 26: 1 ch (does NOT count as st), sc2tog over first 2 sc, 1 sc into each of next 11 sc, sc2tog over next 2 sc, 1 sc into each of next 6 sc, sc2tog over next 2 sc, 1 sc into each of next 11 sc, sc2tog over last 2 sc, ss to first sc, turn: 32 sts.

Round 27: 1 ch (does NOT count as st), 1 sc into each of first 11 sc, sc2tog over next 2 sc, 1 sc into each of next 6 sc, sc2tog over next 2 sc, 1 sc into each of last 11 sc, ss to first sc, turn: 30 sts.

Round 28: 1 ch (does NOT count as st), 1 sc into each of first 11 sc, sc2tog over next 2 sc, 1 sc into each of next 4 sc, sc2tog over next 2 sc, 1 sc into each of last 11 sc, ss to first sc, turn: 28 sts.

Rounds 29 and 30: As round 7.

Now complete bootie by working rounds 35 and 36 as given for hat, noting that there will be 14 ch sps after first of these rounds and 7 patt reps after 2nd of these rounds.

Fasten off.

Finishing

Press carefully following instructions on ball band. Cut ribbon into four 19½ in. (50 cm) lengths (one for each mitten and bootie), leaving 27½ in. (70 cm) for hat. Using photograph as a guide, thread ribbon through ch sps of last-but-one round and tie ends in bow at front.

Pretty in Pink

Roselake is a great color to use for this project as it is a deep pink that is not too pale and pastel as so many yarns for babies seem to be. Cashmere is a wonderful soft yarn to put next to a baby's delicate skin, but it does need extra care when laundering, so follow the instructions on the ball band carefully.

Floppy Rabbit

The body of this rabbit is made of roundels of cream or white yarn in a variety of textures and weights. Designed by Luise Roberts, this is the perfect project to use up your odds and ends or reduce your yarn stash. Use the pattern as a guide but mix and match colors and textures to create your own unique toy.

Materials

Yarn

Handknit Cotton DK by Rowan, 1¾oz/50g ball, each approx 92 yd/85 m (100% cotton)
2 balls in Ecru 251 (A)
1 ball in Sugar 303 (B)

For the body roundels:

Kid Classic by Rowan, 1¾oz/50g ball, each approx 152 yd/140 m (70% lambswool, 26% kid mohair, 4% nylon)
1 ball in Feather 828 (C)
Aran with Wool by Sirdar, 14oz/400g ball, each approx 813 yd/747 m (20% wool, 80% acrylic)
1 ball in Cream 107 (D)
Aqua by Jaeger, 1¾oz/50g ball, each approx 116 yd/106 m (100% cotton)
1 ball in White 300 (E)
Fur by Jaeger, 1¾oz/50g ball, each approx 22 yd/20 m (47% kid mohair, 47% wool, 6% polyamide)
1 ball in Zeal in Polar 048 (F)

Hooks and extras

3.00 mm crochet hook
US 6 (4.00 mm) crochet hook
H/8 (5.00 mm) crochet hook
J/10 (6.00 mm) crochet hook
Washable fiberfill
Large tapestry needle
42 × ⅓ in. (8 mm) glass beads
1 × 1¼ in. (30 mm) round or oval glass bead
2 × ¼ in. (6 mm) buttons in cream
Small amount of blue embroidery floss

Gauge

Head, ears, hands and feet: 20 sts and 20 rows to 4 in. (10 cm) over single crochet pattern, using 3.00 mm hook. Change hook size, if necessary, to obtain this gauge.

Special Abbreviations

pb = place bead
ss tbl = slip stitch through the back loop

Sizes and Measurements

Actual measurements: height 16 in. (40 cm); **each roundel approx** 2¼ in. (6 cm) in diameter, but some variance just adds to the texture and character.

Head

Using 3.00 mm hook and A, ch 5, ss in first ch to form a ring.

Crochet over all yarn ends as you work to reduce the number of ends to weave in at the end. Ch at start of all rounds counts as one st.

Round 1: 2 ch, 8 sc into ring, ss into top of 2 ch: 9 sts.

Round 2: 2 ch, [2 sc into next sc, 1 sc into each of next 2 sc] twice, 2 sc into the next sc, 1 sc into last sc, ss into top of 2 ch: 12 sts.

Round 3: 2 ch, [2 sc into next sc, 1 sc into each of next 2 sc] 3 times, 2 sc into next sc, 1 sc into last sc, ss into top of 2 ch: 16 sts.

Round 4: 2 ch, [2 sc into next sc, 1 sc into each of next 2 sc] 5 times, ss into top of 2 ch: 21 sts.

Round 5: 2 ch, [2 sc into next sc, 1 sc into each of net 2 sc] 6 times, 2 sc into the next sc, 1 sc into last sc, ss into top of 2 ch: 28 sts.

Round 6: 2 ch, 1 sc into each sc, ss into top of 2 ch.

Rep last round 4 times more.

Round 11: 2 ch, 6 hdc, 14 sc, 7 hdc, ss into top of 2 ch.

Round 12: 2 ch, 6 hdc, [2 sc, skip 1 sc] 4 times, 2 sc, 7 hdc, ss into top of 2 ch: 24 sts.

Fill the shape with washable fiberfill.

Round 13: 2 ch, 6 hdc, [1 sc, skip 1 sc] twice, 2 sc, [skip 1 sc, 1 sc] twice, 7 hdc, ss into top of 2 ch: 20 sts.

Round 14: 2 ch, 6 hdc, [1 sc, skip 1 sc] 3 times, 7 hdc, ss into top of 2 ch: 17 sts.

Round 15: 2 ch, [1 sc, skip 1 sc] 8 times, ss into top of 2 ch: 9 sts.

Round 16: 2 ch, [1 sc, skip 1 sc] 4 times, ss into top

of 2 ch: 5 sts.
Fill the shape again with more washable fiberfill.
Fasten off.
Thread end of yarn through each st, draw up tight and secure (this forms end of nose).

Ears (Make 2)
Using 3.00 mm hook and B, ch 32.
Row 1 (RS): Skip 2 ch, 1 sc into each of 18 ch, 1 ss into each of next 12 ch, 1 ss into the start knot, then working back along the other side of the base ch, ss into the next 12 ch, dc into each of 19 ch.
Fasten off B.
Join in A at the point where row 1 starts.
Row 2: ss tbl into each st of first side, [1 ch, 1 ss tbl, 1 ch] in end st, ss tbl into each st to end, turn.
Row 3: 2 ch, working into front loops, work 1 sc into each st to within end st of first side, [1 ch, 1 sc, 1 ch] in end st, 1 sc into each st to end, turn.
Row 4: 3 ch, 1 dc into each st to within end st of first side, [1 ch, 1 sc, 1 ch] in end st, 1 dc into each st to end, turn.
Fold ear in half, WS together, crochet edges together through the inner stitch loops of corresponding sts.
Fasten off.

Hands (Make 2)
Using 3.00mm hook and A, ch 5, ss in first ch to form a ring.
Round 1: 2 ch, 8 sc into ring, ss into top of 2 ch: 9 sts.
Round 2: 2 ch, [2 sc into next st, 1 sc into each of next 2 sc] twice, 2 sc into next sc, 1 sc in last sc, ss into top of 2 ch: 12 sts.
Round 3: 2 ch, [2 sc into the next sc, 1 sc into each of next 2 sc] 3 times, 2 sc into the next sc, 1 sc in last sc, ss into top of 2 ch: 16 sts.
Round 4: 2 ch, 1 sc into each sc, ss into top of 2 ch.
Rep last round 5 times more.

Fill the shape with washable fiberfill.
Round 10: 2 ch, [1 sc into each of 2 sc, skip 1 sc] 5 times, ss into top of 2 ch: 11 sts.
Round 11: 2 ch, [1 sc in next sc, skip 1 sc] 5 times, ss into top of 2 ch: 6 sts.
Fill the shape again with more washable fiberfill, so it is firmly packed.
Fasten off.
Thread end of yarn through each st, draw tight and secure.

Feet (Make 2)
Using 3.00 mm hook and A, ch 5, ss into first ch to form a ring.
Work as hand until round 9 has been worked.
Round 10: 3 ch, 3 hdc, 8 sc, 4 hdc, ss into top of 3 ch.
Rep last round 3 times.
Round 14: 2 ch, 1 sc into each st, ss into top 2 ch.
Rep last round 10 times.
Fill the shape with washable fiberfill.
Round 25: 2 ch, [1 sc into each of 2 sc, skip 1 sc] 5 times, ss into top of 2 ch.
Round 26: 2 ch, [1 sc into next sc, skip 1 sc] 5 times, ss into top of 2 ch.
Fill the shape again with more washable fiberfill, so it is firmly packed.
Fasten off.
Thread end of yarn through each st, draw up tight and secure.

Roundel A (Make 11)
Using H/8 (5.00 mm) hook and C, ch 5, ss into first ch to form a ring.
Round 1: 2 ch, 8 sc ring, ss into top of 2 ch.
Round 2: 3 ch, 2 dc into each st, ss into top of 3 ch.
Round 3: 2 ch, 4 sc into each st.
Cut and finish off yarn by linking into the top of the start chain.

Roundel B (Make 7)

Using US 6 (4.00 mm) hook and A, ch 5, ss into first ch to form a ring.

Rounds 1 and 2: As roundel A.

Round 3: 3 ch, 2 hdc each st.

Cut and finish off yarn by linking into the top of the start chain.

Roundel C (Make 12)

Using a J/10 (6.00 mm) hook and D, ch 4, ss into first ch to form a ring.

Rounds 1 and 2: As roundel A.

Cut and finish off yarn by linking into the top of the start chain.

Roundel D (Make 8)

Using US 6 (4.00 mm) hook and E, ch 4, ss into first ch to form a ring.

Crochet over the yarn ends as you work to reduce the number of ends to weave in at the end.

Work as roundel B.

Roundel E (Make 8)

Using H/8 (5.00 mm) hook and F, ch 5, ss into first ch to form a ring.

Round 1: 3 ch, 8 dc into ring.

Cut and finish off yarn by linking into the top of the start chain.

Finishing

Stitch and weave blue embroidery floss through the holes of each button to form two eyes. Position eyes and secure firmly in place. Split a length of B to two threads and embroider nose and mouth as shown in the photograph. Sew the ears firmly in place.

Threading

Cut four lengths of yarn A, each 25 in. (63 cm) long. Roundels and ⅓ in. (8 mm) beads are threaded on alternately to form the legs, body, arms, and neck.

Legs

Thread two lengths through needle and weave through base chain of one foot piece. Thread roundels and ⅓ in. (8 mm) beads in the following order:

A, pb, B, pb, C, pb, D, pb, A, pb, E, pb, A, pb, D, pb, C, pb, B, pb, E.

Work other leg to match.

Body

Now thread all four lengths through needle and thread on the 1¼ in. (30 mm) bead.

Thread roundels and ⅓ in. (8 mm) beads in the following order:

D, pb, C, pb, B, pb, E, pb, A, pb.

Arms

Now thread 2 lengths through one needle.

Thread roundels and ⅓ in. (8 mm) beads in the following order:

C, pb, A, pb, E, pb, C, pb, D, pb, C, pb, B, pb, A.

Weave yarn around base chain of one hand piece, pass back through roundels and beads of arm.

Work other arm to match with the other two lengths of yarn.

Neck

Now thread all four lengths through one needle and thread on a ⅓ in. (8 mm) bead.

Thread roundels and ⅓ in. (8 mm) beads in the following order:

D, pb, C, pb, E.

Tie a knot firmly in all four lengths of yarn as close as possible to the top of the neck and weave through the base chain of the last roundel.

Secure to the base of the head and weave the threads repeatedly through the head piece embedding it firmly in the fiberfill.

What's up, Doc?

If you start a chain with a backward loop instead of a slip knot it gives a smoother beginning to the chain, which is useful for lace patterns. Try this technique to begin the ears of this Rabbit pattern in order to make working into the start loop a little easier.

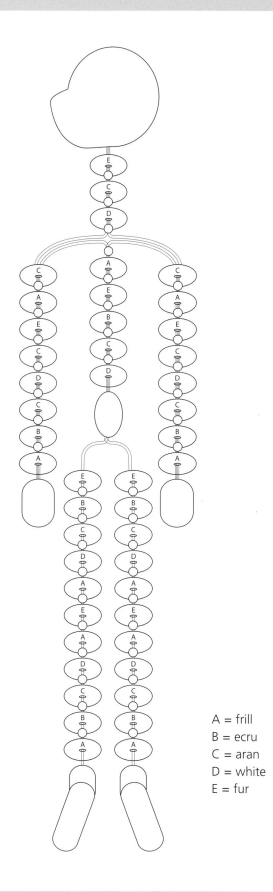

A = frill
B = ecru
C = aran
D = white
E = fur

Daisy Chain Necklace, Bracelet & Hair Clip

*Simple single crochet flowers and bright sparkly yarn are used to make
Sue Whiting's daisy chain jewelry set, which includes a necklace, bracelet and hair
clip. You can make them all in one set of colors—although here we have used a
different color for the hair clip.*

Materials

Yarn
Goldfingering by Twilleys, 1¾oz/50g ball, each
   approx 218 yd/200 m (80% viscose,
   20% metalized polyester)

Necklace
1 ball in red shade 38
1 ball in turquoise shade 53
1 ball in gold shade 2
1 ball in green shade 34

Bracelet
Oddments in red shade 38, gold shade 2 and green
   shade 34

Hair Clip
Oddments in white shade 10 and burnt orange
   shade 64

Hooks and extras
2.00 mm crochet hook
Hair clip

Gauge
24 sts and 27 rows to 4 in. (10 cm) measured over
   single crochet fabric using 2.00 mm hook.
   Change hook size, if necessary, to obtain this
   gauge.

Actual measurements: flower diameter 2¾ in. (7 cm); **necklace length** 49¼ in. (125 cm); **bracelet length** 7¾ in. (20 cm)

Flower Petals (Make 5 for each flower)
With 2.00 mm hook and petal color, ch 2.
Round 1 (RS): 6 sc into 2nd ch from hook, ss to first sc, turn: 6 sts.
Round 2: 1 ch (does NOT count as st), 2 sc into first sc, 1 sc into next sc, 2 sc into each of next 2 sc, 1 sc into next sc, 2 sc into last sc, ss to first sc, turn: 10 sts.

Round 3: 1 ch (does NOT count as st), 2 sc into first sc, 1 sc into each of next 3 sc, 2 sc into each of next

2 sc, 1 sc into each of next 3 sc, 2 sc into last sc, ss to first sc, turn: 14 sts.

Round 4: 1 ch (does NOT count as st), 1 sc into each sc to end, ss to first sc, turn.

Rounds 5 and 6: As round 4.

Round 7: 1 ch (does NOT count as st), sc2tog over first 2 sc, 1 sc into each of next 3 sc, [sc2tog over next 2 sc] twice, 1 sc into each of next 3 sc, sc2tog over last 2 sc, ss to first sc, turn: 10 sts.

Round 8: As round 4.

Fasten off.

Fold petal flat so the tops of last round meet.

Make flower center:

With 2.00 mm hook and center color, ch 2.

Round 1 (RS): 5 sc into 2nd ch from hook, ss to first sc, turn: 5 sts.

Round 2: 1 ch (does NOT count as st), 3 sc into each sc to end, ss to first sc, turn: 15 sts.

Round 3: 1 ch (does NOT count as st), 1 sc into each sc, working through top of last round of Petal at same time—work 3 sc across base of each Petal, thereby attaching 5 Petals all around, ss to first sc, turn.

Round 4: 1 ch (does NOT count as st), [sc2tog over next 2 sc] 7 times, 1 sc into last sc, ss to first sc, turn: 8 sts.

Round 5: 1 ch (does NOT count as st), [sc2tog over next 2 sc] 4 times, ss to first sc.

Fasten off.

Necklace

Make 10 flowers, using red for petals of 5 flowers and turquoise for petals of other 5 flowers, and gold for all flower centers.

Make chain:

With 2.00 mm hook and green, ch 2, 1 sc into 2nd ch from hook, *insert hook into left side strand of st just worked, yarn over hook and draw loop through, yarn over hook and draw through 2 loops, rep from

* until chain is approx 49¼ in. (125 cm) long.
Fasten off.

Bracelet

Using red for petals and gold for flower center, make
one flower.

Make chain:

With 2.00 mm hook and green, ch 2, 1 sc into 2nd ch
from hook, *insert hook into left side strand of st just
worked, yarn over hook and draw loop through, yarn
over hook and draw through 2 loops, rep from * until
chain is approx 7¾ in. (20 cm) long.
Fasten off.

Hair Pin

Using white for petals and burnt orange for flower
center, make one flower.

Finishing

To make up necklace, join ends of chain, then sew
flowers to chain every 5 in. (12.5 cm), alternating
colors of flowers.
To make up bracelet, join ends of chain, then sew
flower to chain over join.
Attach flower to hair clip.

Flower Power

You will not use the full amount of yarn specified
in the pattern for the necklace, so you can use
the leftover yarn for the bracelet and hair clip and
have a matching set.

Make sets of each item to match every outfit in
your child's wardrobe and never be without the
right accessory again!

Instead of a hair clip, you could attach the single
flower to a hair scrunchie or headband for a
slightly different look.

One or two flowers stitched to a safety pin would
also make a great corsage to brighten up a plain
dress or coat.

Granny-Square Baby Blanket

Sophie Britten's delightful checkerboard baby cot or stroller afghan is composed of traditional granny squares in delicious fruity colors. This afghan is made up of 49 squares arranged 7 by 7 in a square shape, but if you need a bigger size or a rectangular shape, just add more squares!

Materials

Yarn

RYC Cashsoft DK by Rowan, 1¾oz/50g ball, each approx 142 yd/130 m (57% extra fine merino wool, 33% microfiber, 10% cashmere)

1 ball in Sweet
1 ball in Bella Donna
1 ball in Ballad Blue
1 ball in Limone
4 balls in Lime

Hooks and extras

E/4 (3.5 mm) crochet hook

Gauge

Each square should measure 3½ × 3½ in. (9 × 9 cm). Change hook size if necessary to achieve this gauge.

Sizes and Measurements

Actual measurements: afghan 25 × 25 in. (64 × 64 cm) square; **each square** 3½ × 3½ in. (9 × 9 cm)

Multicolor squares

Make 24 squares using several different combinations of shades Sweet, Bella Donna, Ballad Blue and Limone.

Using color A, ch 4, join in a ring with a ss.

Round 1: 3 ch (count as 1 dc), 2 dc into ring, 1ch, work (3 dc into ring, 1 ch) 3 times, ss in top of 3 ch: 16 sts.
Fasten off.

Round 2: Join color B to same place as ss, 3 ch (count as 1 dc), 1 dc into each of the next 2 sts. *(2 dc, 1ch, 2 dc) into ch sp, 1 dc into each of next 3 sts; repeat from * twice more, (2 dc, 1 ch, 2 dc) into last ch sp, ss into top of 3 ch: 32 sts.
Fasten off.

Round 3: Join color C to same place as ss, 3 ch, 1 dc into each of next 4 sts *(2 dc, 1 ch, 2 dc) into ch sp, 1 dc into each of next 7 sts; repeat from * twice more, (2 dc, 1 ch, 2 dc) into last ch sp, 1 dc into each

of next 2 sts, ss in top of 3 ch: 48 sts.
Fasten off.

Round 4: Join color D to same place as ss, 3 ch, 1 dc into each of next 6 sts *(2 dc, 1 ch, 2 dc) into ch sp, 1 dc into each of next 11 sts; repeat from * twice more, (2 dc, 1 ch, 2 dc) into last ch sp, 1 dc into each of next 4 sts, ss in top of 3 ch: 64 sts.
Fasten off.

Plain color squares

Make 25 squares in Lime, working as above without fastening off after each round.

Finishing

Block each square so the sides are straight and press gently. Arrange the squares in 7 rows of 7 squares, alternating one plain Lime color square and one multicolored square, placing a plain Lime square at each corner of the afghan. Join squares by placing wrong sides together, align the stitches and work in single crochet under both strands of edge stitches of each square. When all the squares have been joined, work 1 round of sc in Lime around the edge of the afghan working 3 sc into 1 ch sp at each corner.

Tip

For a different look, try making the blanket either all in plain squares or all in multicolor squares. This design is based on using repeating square motifs in exactly the same design. Try creating your own unique afghan by using one of the alternative square motifs featured on page 166.

If you are making this afghan for a nursery, make some extra squares and make a matching cushion for the nursery chair as well. For an 18 in. (45 cm) square pillow form, make 12 multicolor squares and 13 plain squares for the front, and 25 plain squares for the back of the cover. Arrange the squares for the front cover in 5 rows of 5 squares, alternating one plain Lime color square and one multicolored square, placing a plain Lime square at each corner of the cushion cover. Join and work the edging as for the afghan, then join the 25 squares for the back and edge in the same way. Join the front and back together with single crochet (see page 50) around three sides. Insert the pillow form, then sew snap fastenings on the last side to close.

Alternatively, work 6 short lengths of single crochet chain as described on page 78 to make three pairs of tie fastenings. Stitch one tie between 1st and 2nd squares at each end of one side and one in the center, stitch the other three in matching positions on other side, then tie each pair in an attractive bow to close the cushion.

Stitch Library

Now that you've mastered the basic techniques, your crochet has reached an entirely new level where you can alter existing patterns or even create your own designs. Try adding a pretty crochet edging to a plain garment, or using a lacy stitch for the fabric instead of a plain one. This chapter provides you with some beginner and advanced stitches to experiment with—so you are only limited by your own creativity.

Stitch Library

All-Over Patterns

Basic Single Crochet

Starting chain: any number of sts
  + 1
Drape: good
Skill: easy

Row 1: Skip 2 ch (count as 1 sc),
  1 sc into next and each ch to
  end, turn.

Row 2: 1 ch (counts as 1 sc), skip
  1 st, 1 sc into next and each st
  to end, working last st into tch,
  turn.
Rep row 2.
Hint: In some patterns the turning
  chain does not count as a stitch
  when working single crochet. In
  these cases the first sc is worked
  into the 2nd ch from hook on
  the first row, and thereafter into
  the first sc of the previous row.

Basic Half Double

Starting chain: any number of sts
  + 1
Drape: good
Skill: easy

Row 1: Skip 2 ch (count as
  1 hdc), 1 hdc into next and
  each ch to end, turn.
Row 2: 2 ch (count as 1 hdc),
  skip 1 st, 1 hdc into next and
  each st to end working last st
  into top of tch, turn.
Rep row 2.

Basic Double

Starting chain: any number of sts
  + 2
Drape: good
Skill: easy

Row 1: Skip 3 ch (count as
  1 dc), 1 dc into next and each
  ch to end, turn.
Row 2: 3 ch (count as 1 dc), skip
  1 st, 1 dc into next and each st
  to end working last st into top
  of tch, turn.
Rep row 2.

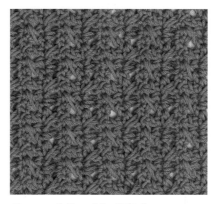

Basic Treble

Starting chain: any number of sts + 3
Drape: good
Skill: easy

Row 1: Skip 4 ch (count as 1 tr), 1 tr into next and each ch to end, turn.
Row 2: 4 ch (count as 1 tr), skip 1 st, 1 tr into next and each st to end working last st into top of tch, turn.
Rep row 2.

Crossed Double Stitch

Starting chain: multiple of 2 sts + 2
Drape: excellent
Skill: intermediate

Special abbreviation
2Cdc (2 Crossed Doubles)—skip next st, 1 dc into next st, 1 dc into skipped st working over previous dc.
Row 1 (RS): Skip 3 ch (count as 1 dc), *2Cdc over next 2 ch; rep from * ending 1 dc into last ch, turn.
Row 2: 1 ch (counts as 1 sc), skip 1 st, 1 sc into next and each st to end, working last st into top of tch, turn.
Row 3: 3 ch (counts as 1 dc), skip 1 st, *work 2Cdc over next 2 sts; rep from * ending 1 dc into tch, turn.
Rep rows 2 and 3.

Crossbill Stitch

Starting chain: multiple of 4 sts + 3
Drape: excellent
Skill: intermediate

Special abbreviation
2dcC (2 Doubles Crossed)—skip 2 sts, 1 dc into next st, 1 ch, 1 dc into first of 2 sts just skipped working back over last dc made.

Row 1: Skip 3 ch (count as 1 dc), *work 2dcC over next 3 ch, 1 dc into next ch; rep from * to end, turn.
Row 2: 3 ch (count as 1 dc), 1 dc into first st, skip 1 dc, *1 dc into next ch, work 2dcC over next 3 dc, rep from * ending 1 dc into last ch, skip 1 dc, 2 dc into top of tch, turn.
Row 3: 3 ch (count as 1 dc), skip 1 st, *work 2dcC over next 3 dc, 1 dc into next ch; rep from * ending last rep into top of tch, turn.
Rep rows 2 and 3.

Lace patterns

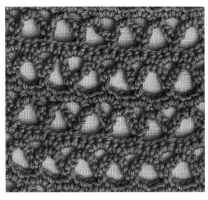

Sedge Stitch
Starting chain: multiple of 3 sts +
3
Drape: good
Skill: easy

Row 1: Skip 2 ch (count as 1 sc),
work [1 hdc, 1 dc] into next ch,
*skip 2 ch, work [1 sc, 1 hdc,
1 dc] into next ch; rep from * to
last 3 ch, skip 2 ch, 1 sc into
last ch, turn.
Row 2: 1 ch (counts as 1 sc),
work [1 hdc, 1 dc] into first st,
*skip [1 dc and 1 hdc], work
[1 sc, 1 hdc, 1 dc] into next sc;
rep from * to last 3 sts, skip
[1 dc and 1 hdc], 1 sc into top
of tch, turn.
Rep row 2.

Silt Stitch
Starting chain: multiple of 3 sts +
3
Drape: good
Skill: easy

Row 1 (RS): Skip 3 ch (count as
1 dc), 1 dc into next and each
ch to end, turn.
Row 2: 1 ch (counts as 1 sc),
2 dc into first st, *skip 2 sts,
work [1 sc, 2 dc] into next st;
rep from * to last 3 sts, skip 2
sts, 1 sc into top of tch, turn.
Row 3: 3 ch (counts as 1 dc), skip
1 st, 1 dc into next and each st
to end, working last st into top
of tch, turn.
Rep rows 2 and 3.

Ruled Lattice
Starting chain: multiple of 4 sts +
2
Drape: excellent
Skill: easy

Row 1 (RS): 1 sc into 2nd ch
from hook, 1 sc into each ch to
end, turn.
Row 2: 7 ch, skip first 2 sts, 1 sc
into next st, *7 ch, skip 3 sts,
1 sc into next st; rep from * to
last 2 sts, 3 ch, skip 1 st, 1 dc
into last st, skip tch, turn.
Row 3: 1 ch, 1 sc into first st,
*3 ch, 1 sc into next 7 ch arch;
rep from * to end, turn.
Row 4: 1 ch, 1 sc into first st,
*3 sc into next 3 ch arch, 1 sc
into next sc; rep from * to end,
skip tch, turn.
Rep rows 2, 3 and 4.

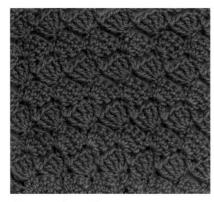

Acrobatic Stitch

Starting chain: multiple of 6 sts + 3
Drape: excellent
Skill: intermediate

Row 1 (RS): 2 dc into 3rd ch from hook, *4 ch, skip 5 ch, 5 dc into ch: rep from * working only 3 dc at end of last rep, turn.

Row 2: 2 ch (counts as 1 dc), skip first 3 sts, *work [3 dc, 3 ch, 3 dc] into next 4 ch arch**, skip next 5 dc; rep from * ending last rep at **, skip 2dc, 1dc into top of tch, turn.

Row 3: 6 ch (counts as 1 dtr and 1 ch), *5 dc into next 3 ch arch**, 4 ch; rep from * ending last rep at **, 1 ch, 1 dtr into top of tch, turn.

Row 4: 5 ch (counts as 1 tr and 1 ch), 3 dc into next 1 ch sp, *skip 5 dc, work [3 dc, 3 ch, 3 dc] into next 4 ch arch; rep from * ending skip 5 dc, work [3 dc, 1 ch, 1 tr] into tch, turn.

Row 5: 3ch (counts as 1 dc), 2 dc into next 1 ch sp, *4 ch, 5 dc into next 3 ch arch; rep from * ending 4 ch, 3 dc into tch, turn.
Rep rows 2, 3, 4 and 5.

Shell Trellis

Starting chain: multiple of 12 sts + 3
Drape: excellent
Skill: intermediate

Row 1 (RS): 2 dc into 3rd ch from hook, *skip 2 ch, 1 sc into next ch, 5 ch, skip 5 ch, 1 sc into next ch, skip 2 ch, 5 dc into next ch; rep from * ending last rep with 3 dc into last ch, turn.

Row 2: 1 ch, 1 sc into first st, *5 ch, 1 sc into next 5 ch arch, 5 ch, 1 sc into 3rd dc of next 5 dc; rep from * ending last rep with 1 sc into top of tch, turn.

Row 3: *5 ch, 1 sc in next 5 ch arch, 5 dc into next sc, 1 sc into next arch; rep from * ending 2 ch, 1 dc into last sc, skip tch, turn.

Row 4: 1 ch, 1 sc into first st, *5 ch, 1 sc into 3rd dc of next 5 dc, 5 ch, 1 sc into next 5 ch arch; rep from * to end, turn.

Row 5: 3 ch (counts as 1 dc), 2 dc into first st, *1 sc into next arch, 5 ch, 1 sc into next arch, 5 dc into next sc; rep from * ending last rep with only 3 dc into last sc, skip tch, turn.
Rep rows 2, 3, 4 and 5.

Alternating Clusters

Starting chain: multiple of 4 sts + 4
Drape: excellent
Skill: easy

Row 1 (RS): Work 4 dc into 4th ch from hook, skip 3 ch, 1 sc into next ch, *2 ch, 4 dc into same ch as last sc, skip 3 ch, 1 sc into next ch; rep from * to end, turn.

Row 2: 5 ch, work 4 dc into 4th ch from hook, *skip 4 dc, 1 sc between last dc skipped and next 2 ch, 2 ch, 4 dc into side of last sc worked; rep from * to last 4 dc, skip 4 dc, 1 sc into next ch, turn.
Rep row 2.

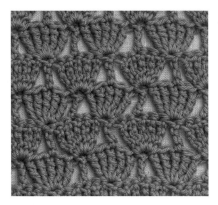

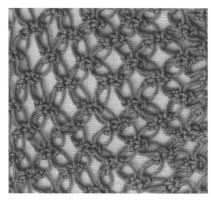

Palm Pattern

Starting chain: multiple of 8 sts +
     12
Drape: excellent
Skill: easy

Row 1 (RS): Work 5 tr into 8th
   ch from hook, skip 3 ch, 1 tr
   into next ch, *skip 3 ch, 5 tr
   into next ch, skip 3 ch, 1 tr into
   next ch; rep from * to end,
   turn.
Row 2: 4 ch (counts as 1 tr), 2 tr
   into first tr, skip 2 tr, 1 tr into
   next tr, *skip 2 tr, 5 tr into next
   tr, skip 2 tr, 1 tr into next tr; rep
   from * to last 3 sts, skip
   2 tr, 3 tr into next ch, turn.
Row 3: 4 ch, *skip 2 tr, 5 tr into
   next tr, skip 2 tr, 1 tr into next
   tr; rep from * to end placing
   last tr into 4th of 4 ch at beg of
   previous row, turn.
Rep rows 2 and 3.

Picot Fan Stitch

Starting chain: multiple of 12 sts
     + 2
Drape: excellent
Skill: intermediate

Row 1 (RS): 1 sc into 2nd ch
   from hook, *5 ch, skip 3 ch,
   1 sc into next ch; rep from * to
   end, turn.
Row 2: 5 ch (counts as 1 dc and
   2 ch), *1 sc into next 5 ch arch,
   8 dc into next arch, 1 sc into
   next arch**, 5 ch; rep from *
   ending last rep at ** in last
   arch, 2 ch, 1 dc into last sc, skip
   tch, turn.
Row 3: 1 ch, 1 sc into first st,
   skip 2 ch and 1 sc, *work a
   Picot of [1 dc into next dc,
   3 ch, insert hook down through
   top of dc just made and ss to
   close] 7 times, 1 dc into next dc,
   1 sc into next arch; rep from *
   to end, turn.
Row 4: 8 ch, skip 2 Picots, *1 sc
   into next Picot, 5 ch, skip 1
   Picot, 1 sc into next Picot, 5 ch,
   skip 2 Picots, 1 dc into next
   sc**, 5 ch, skip 2 Picots; rep
   from * ending last rep at **,
   skip tch, turn.
Rep rows 2, 3 and 4.

Solomon's Knot

Starting chain: multiple of 2
     Solomon's Knots + 1
Drape: excellent
Skill: intermediate

Special abbreviation
ESK (Edge Solomon's Knot)—
   these form the base "chain"
   and edges of the fabric and are
   two-3rds the length of MSKs.
MSK (Main Solomon's Knot)—
   these form the main fabric and
   are half as long again as ESKs.
Base "chain": 2 ch, 1 sc into 2nd
   ch from hook, now make a
   multiple of 2ESKs (say ¾in./
   2 cm), ending with 1MSK (say
   1⅛ in./3 cm)

Row 1: 1 sc into sc between 3rd
   and 4th loops from hook,
   *2MSK, skip 2 loops, 1 sc into
   next sc; rep from * to end, turn.
Row 2: 2ESK and 1MSK, 1 sc into
   sc between 4th and 5th loops
   from hook, *2MSK, skip 2
   loops, 1 sc into next sc; rep
   from * ending in top of ESK,
   turn.
Rep row 2.

Motifs

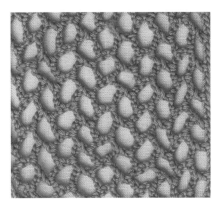

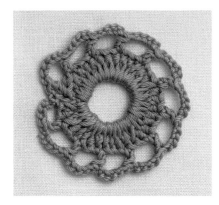

Plain trellis

Starting chain: multiple of 4 sts + 6

Drape: excellent

Skill: easy

Row 1: 1 sc into 6th ch from hook, *5 ch, skip 3 ch, 1 sc into next ch; rep from * to end, turn.

Row 2: *5 ch, 1 sc into next 5ch arch; rep from * to end, turn.

Rep row 2.

Little Flower

Skill: intermediate

Special abbreviation

Dc2tog—work 1 dc into each of next 2 sc until 1 loop of each remains on hook, yo and through all 3 loops on hook.

Make 6 ch, ss into first ch to form a ring.

Round 1: 1 ch, work 15 sc into ring, ss into first sc.

Round 2: [3 ch, dc2tog over next 2 sc, 3 ch, ss into next sc] 5 times placing last ss into last sc of previous round.

Fasten off.

Sun Star

Skill: intermediate

Make 16 ch, ss into first ch to form a ring.

Round 1: 2 ch (counts as 1 hdc), work 35 hdc into ring and over padding threads, ss into 2nd of 2 ch at beg of round.

Round 2: 1 ch, work 1 sc into same st as last ss, [5 ch, skip 2 hdc, 1 sc into next hdc] 11 times, 5 ch, ss into first sc.

Fasten off.

Daisy

Skill: easy

Make 6ch, ss into first ch to form a ring and continue as follows: 1ch, work [1sc, 12ch] 12 times into ring, ss into first sc.

Fasten off.

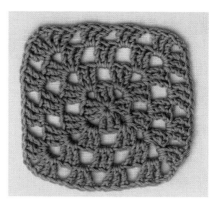

Popcorn Wheel Square

Skill: intermediate

Note: For detail steps of Popcorn see page 42.

Make 6ch, ss into first ch to form a ring.

Round 1: 3 ch (counts as 1 dc), 4 dc into ring and complete as for 5 dc Popcorn, [3 ch, 5 dc Popcorn into ring] 7 times, 3 ch, ss to first Popcorn.

Round 2: 3 ch (count as 1 dc), 1 dc into next 3 ch arch, [9 dc into next arch, 2 dc into next arch] 3 times, 9 dc into last arch, ss to top of 3 ch.

Round 3: 1 ch, 1 sc into same place as 1 ch, 1 sc into next st, *into next 9 dc group work 1 sc into each of first 3 dc, skip 1 dc, [1 hdc, 4 dc, 1 hdc] into next dc, skip 1 dc, 1 sc into each of last 3 dc**, 1 sc into each of next 2 sts; rep from * twice and from * to ** again, ss to first sc.

Fasten off.

Traditional Square

Skill: intermediate

Make 4 ch, ss into first ch to form a ring.

Round 1: 5 ch (counts as 1 dc and 2 ch), [3 dc into ring, 2 ch] 3 times, 2 dc into ring, ss to 3rd of 5 ch.

Round 2: Ss into next ch, 5 ch (counts as 1 dc and 2 ch), 3 dc into same sp, *1 ch, skip 3 dc, [3 dc, 2 ch, 3 dc] into next sp; rep from * twice, 1 ch, skip 3 sts, 2 dc into same sp as 5 ch at beg of round, ss to 3rd of 5ch.

Round 3: Ss into next ch, 5 ch (counts as 1 dc and 2 ch], 3 dc into same sp, *1 ch, skip 3 dc, 3 dc into next sp, 1 ch, skip 3 dc**, [3 dc, 2 ch, 3 dc] into next sp; rep from * twice then from * to **, 2 dc into same sp as 5 ch, ss to 3rd of 5 ch.

Round 4: Ss into next ch, 5 ch (counts as 1 dc and 2 ch), 3 dc into same sp, *[1 ch, skip 3 dc, 3 dc into next sp] twice, 1 ch, skip 3 dc**, [3 dc, 2 ch, 3 dc] into next sp; rep from * twice and from * to ** again, 2 dc into same sp as 5 ch, ss to 3rd of 5 ch.

Fasten off.

Sow Thistle Square

Skill: intermediate

Special abbreviations

Dc2tog—*yarn over hook, insert hook into next stitch, yarn over hook, draw a loop through, yarn over hook and draw through 2 loops on hook** (2 loops on hook); rep from * to ** into next stitch (3 loops on hook). Yarn over hook and draw through all loops to complete stitch.

Dc3tog—*yarn over hook, insert hook into next stitch, yarn over hook, draw a loop through, yarn over hook and draw through 2 loops on hook (2 loops on hook); rep from * to ** into next stitch (3 loops on hook); rep from * to ** again into next stitch (4 loops on hook). Yarn over hook and draw through all loops to complete stitch.

Using Yarn A, make 4 ch, ss into first ch.

Round 1: 4ch (counts as 1dc and 1ch), [1dc, 1ch] 11 times into ring, ss to 3rd of 4ch.

Fasten off: 12 sps.

Round 2: Using Yarn B, join into
  sp, 3 ch, dc2tog into same sp
  (counts as dc3tog), [3 ch,
  dc3tog into next sp] 11 times,
  3 ch, ss to top of first Cluster.
Fasten off.
Round 3: Using Yarn A, join
  into 3 ch arch, 1 ch, 1 sc into
  same arch, [5 ch, 1 sc into next
  arch] 11 times, 2 ch, 1 dc into
  first sc.
Fasten off.
Round 2: Using Yarn B, join into
  same place, 1 ch, 1 sc into same
  place, *5 ch, 1 sc into next
  arch, 1 ch, [5 dc, 3 ch,
  5 dc] into next arch, 1 ch, 1 sc
  into next arch; rep from * 3
  times, omitting 1 sc at end of
  last rep, ss to first sc.
Fasten off.

Six-Petal Flower
Skill: easy

Special abbreviation
Bobble—work 5 dc into next sc
  until 1 loop of each remains on
  hook, yo and through all 6
  loops on hook.
Make 6 ch, ss into first ch to form
  a ring.
Round 1: 1 ch, work 12 sc into
  ring, ss into first sc.
Round 2: 3 ch, work 4 dc into
  same st as last ss until 1 loop of
  each dc remains on hook, yo
  and through all 5 loops on hook
  (1 Bobble made at beg of
  round), *5 ch, skip 1 sc, 1
  Bobble into next sc; rep from *
  4 times more, 5 ch, ss into top
  of first Bobble.
Fasten off.

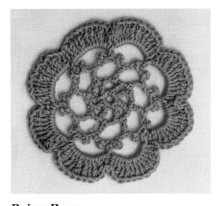

Briar Rose
Skill: intermediate

Using Yarn A, make 3ch, ss into
  first ch.
Round 1: 5 ch (counts as 1 dc
  and 2 ch), [1 dc into ring, 2 ch]
  7 times, ss to 3rd of 5 ch.
Fasten off: 8 sps.
Round 2: Join Yarn B into a sp, 9
  ch, ss into 4th ch from hook, 5
  ch, ss into 4th ch from hook, 1
  ch, *1 dc into next sp, work a
  Picot of [5 ch, ss into 4th ch
  from hook] twice, 1 ch; rep
  from * six times more, ss to 3rd
  ch of starting ch.
Fasten off.
Round 3: Join Yarn C into 1 ch
  between 2 Picots, 1 ch, 1 sc
  into same place as 1 ch, *7 ch,
  skip [1 Picot, 1 dc and 1 Picot],
  1 sc into next ch between
  Picots; rep from * 7 times more
  omitting sc at end of last rep, ss
  to first sc.
Round 4: Ss into next ch, 1 ch,
  *work [1 sc, 1 hdc, 9 dc, 1 hdc,
  1 sc] into next arch; rep from *
  7 times more, ss to first sc.
Fasten off.

Edgings

Shell edging
Multiple of 4 sts + 1
Skill: easy

Row 1 (RS): 1 sc, *skip 1 st or equivalent interval, 5 dc into next st, skip 1 st, 1 sc into next st; rep from *.
Fasten off.

Picot Edging
Multiple of 2 sts + 1
Skill: easy

Row 1 (RS): 1 sc, *3 ch, ss into 3rd ch from hook, skip 1 st or equivalent interval, 1 sc into next st; rep from *.
Fasten off.

Simple Scallop Edging
Starting chain: multiple of 4 sts + 2
Skill: easy

Row 1 (RS): Work 1 sc into 2nd ch from hook, 1 sc into each ch to end, turn.
Row 2: 1 ch, 1 sc into first sc, *5 ch, skip 3 sc, 1 sc into next sc; rep from * to end, turn.
Row 3: 1 ch, 1 sc into first sc, *7 ch, 1 sc into next sc; rep from * to end.
Fasten off.

Arch & Picot Edging
Starting chain: multiple of 5 sts + 1
Skill: intermediate

Row 1 (RS): Work 1 sc into 2nd ch from hook, 1 sc into each ch to end, turn.
Row 2: 1 ch, 1 sc into first sc, *5 ch, ss into 3rd ch from hook, 3 ch, skip next 4 sc, 1 sc into next sc; rep from * to end, turn.
Row 3: 1 ch, 1 sc into first sc, *6 ch, ss into 3rd ch from hook, 4ch, 1 sc into next sc; rep from * to end.
Fasten off.

Shallow Scallop Edging
Starting chain: multiple of 6 sts + 3
Skill: intermediate

Row 1 (WS): Work 1 sc into 2nd ch from hook, 1 sc into each ch to end, turn.
Row 2: 3 ch (counts as 1 dc), skip first sc, 1 dc into next sc, *1 ch, skip 1 sc, 1 dc into each of next 2 sc; rep from * to end, turn.
Row 3: 5 ch (counts as 1 dc, 2 ch), 1 sc into next ch sp, *4 ch, 1 sc into next ch sp; rep from * to last 2 sts, 2 ch, 1 dc into 3rd of 3 ch at beg of previous row, turn.
Row 4: 1 ch, 1 sc into first dc, *work 5 dc into next 4 ch sp, 1 sc into next 4 ch sp; rep from * to end placing last sc into 3rd of 5 ch at beg of previous row.
Fasten off.

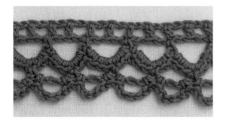

Aqueduct Edging
Starting chain: multiple of 4 sts +
4
Skill: intermediate

Row 1 (RS): Work 1 dc into 6th
ch from hook, *1 ch, skip 1 ch,
1 dc into next ch; rep from * to
end, turn.

Row 2: 1 ch, 1 sc into first dc,
*5 ch, skip 1 dc, 1 sc into next
dc; rep from * to last dc, 5 ch,
skip 1 dc and 1 ch, 1 sc into
next ch, turn.

Row 3: 1 ch, 1 sc into first sc,
work 7 sc into each 5 ch arch to
end, 1 sc into last sc, turn.

Row 4: 5 ch (counts as 1 dc, 2
ch), skip first 4 sc, 1 sc into next
sc, *3 ch, skip 6 sc, 1 sc into
next sc; rep from * to last 4 sc,
2 ch, 1 dc into last sc, turn.

Row 5: 1 ch, 1 sc into first dc,
5 ch, 1 sc into 2 ch sp, into
each sp work [1 sc, 5 ch, 1 sc]
to end placing last sc into 3rd of
5 ch at beg of previous row.
Fasten off.

Soft Slope Edging
Starting chain: multiple of 6 sts +
3
Skill: intermediate

Special abbreviation
Picot—make 3 ch, ss into 3rd ch
from hook.

Row 1 (WS): Work 1 sc into 2nd
ch from hook, 1 sc into each ch
to end, turn.

Row 2: 5 ch (counts as 1 dc,
2 ch), skip first 3 sc, 1 sc into
next sc, work 3 Picots, 1 sc into
next sc, *5 ch, skip 4 sc, 1 sc
into next sc, work 3 Picots, 1 sc
into next sc; rep from * to last 3
sc, 2 ch, 1 dc into last sc, turn.

Row 3: 1 ch, 1 sc into first dc,
*8 ch, 1 sc into next 5 ch arch;
rep from *to end placing last sc
into 3rd of 5 ch at beg of
previous row, turn.

Row 4: 1 ch, 1 sc into first sc,
*11 sc into next 3 ch arch, 1 sc
into next sc; rep from * to end.
Fasten off.

Spiked Edging
Worked lengthways
Skill: intermediate

Row 1 (RS): Make 14 ch, work
1 sc into 3rd ch from hook,
1 hdc into next ch, 1 dc into
next ch, 1 tr into next ch, [1 ch,
skip 1 ch, 1 tr into next ch]
twice, 2 ch, skip 2 ch, 1 tr into
each of last 2 ch, turn.

Row 2: 1 ch, 1 sc into each of
first 2 tr, 1 sc into 2 ch sp, 4 ch,
1 sc into same sp as last sc, 1 dc
into next tr, 1 sc into ch sp, 1 sc
into next tr, turn.

Row 3: 7 ch, work 1 sc into 3rd
ch from hook, 1 hdc into next
ch, 1 dc into next ch, 1 tr into
next ch, 1 ch, 1 tr into next sc,
1 ch, skip 1 sc, 1 tr into next sc,
2 ch, skip 2 sc, 1 tr into each of
last 2 sc, turn.
Rep rows 2 and 3.
Fasten off.

Aftercare

*After spending so much time, care and attention creating your hand-crocheted
item, you will want to care for it properly so that it will last for years to come. Hand-made
items will not stand repeat washing as well as machine-made ones, but as long as you
follow some basic rules they should still be fine. First read the information on the
recommended cleaning for the yarn, which you will find on the ball band. It is a good
idea to keep a length of the yarn you have used and one ball band—the yarn will be
useful if you do have to repair something, and the ball band will be
a reference for cleaning instructions in the future.*

Storage
Store crocheted items folded on a shelf, or in a closed drawer, if possible. Never hang on hangers, as they will stretch out of shape. If an item will be stored for some time, make sure it is clean and dry and pack in a large plastic bag. Use a proper repellent in the storage space to keep moths away—natural materials such as cedar wood can be effective, or use chemical strips or mothballs.

Hand-washing
Use lukewarm water and a mild detergent specially formulated for knitted or crochet items. Keep the item under water and squeeze gently all over to clean—do not lift it out of the water, which may stretch it, or rub, which may damage the surface of the yarn or pull stitches. Let the water out, squeezing gently to remove as much water trapped in the yarn as possible. Rinse several times in lukewarm water, then again squeeze gently to remove as much water as possible. Do not wring, just press and squeeze. Some yarns my be suitable for tumble-drying—check the ball band. If not, lay the item out on a clean, colorfast towel and pull it gently into shape. Leave it

to dry away from direct heat. If necessary, iron when dry following the instructions on page 49.

Machine Washing
Some yarns are suitable for machine washing—check the ball band. Choose a program that matches the symbols on the ball band and stick to the recommended water temperature. It can be a good idea to wash large items inside a colorfast bag such as a pillowcase, as this will keep them confined and less likely to stretch. Remove the item from the machine as soon as the cycle finishes and leave it to dry as described above.

Dry cleaning
If the ball band says the yarn can be dry cleaned, make sure the dry cleaner is aware of the symbols given as these indicate which chemicals should be used. Do not dry clean items that can be washed—it will not prolong their life and the chemicals may be harmful to the yarn. Ask the dry cleaner not to hang the item on a hanger, or to iron it.

Abbreviations

alt	alt		**rep**	repeat
approx	approximately		**RS**	right side
beg	beginning		**sc**	single crochet
ch	chain(s)		**sc2tog**	single crochet two stitches together
ch sp	chain space(s)		**sk**	skip
cm	centimeter		**sp**	space(s)
cont	continue		**ss2tog**	slip stitch two stitches together
dc	double crochet		**ss**	slip st
dc2tog	double crochet two stitches together		**st(s)**	stitch(es)
dc3tog	double crochet three stitches together		**tch**	turning chain
dec	decrease		**tog**	together
dtr	double treble		**tr**	treble
foll	following		**trtr**	triple treble
hdc	half double crochet		**WS**	wrong side
in	inch(es)		**yd**	yard
inc	increase		**yo**	yarn over hook (US)
m	meters		**yrh**	yarn around hook
oz	ounce		**[ ]**	work instructions in square brackets as directed
patt(s)	pattern(s)			
rem	remaining			

Glossary of Crochet Terms

Afghan crochet—see Tunisian crochet.

Bobble—a cluster of stitches (usually three to five) worked in the same place and joined together at the top (unlike those of a popcorn, which are separated).

Broomstick lace—a form of crochet using a very thick "broomstick" needle and a crochet hook to make a very open-textured fabric.

Cluster—two or more stitches joined together at the top. Any combination of stitches may be joined into a cluster by leaving the last loop of each temporarily on the hook and taking them all off together at the end.

Damp finishing—a method of flattening and pulling into shape without steam pressing. It is used for synthetic yarns and highly textured work.

Dye lot—a number given to each dye batch of yarn in the same shade.

Filet crochet—an early traditional form of crochet worked with a fine hook and cotton thread, producing a fabric resembling bobbin lace, see page 45.

Foundation chain—the first length of chain stitch made with the required number of chains for the first row of crochet, plus any extra needed to allow for the height of the stitch being worked, see page 35.

Loop stitch—a variation of single crochet worked on wrong side rows so loops form on the front of the fabric, see page 43.

Motif—a crochet shape, which may be a circle, square, hexagon or other geometric shape. The motifs can be joined together in different combinations to create an open fabric.

Ply—the term for the strands of fiber that make up a yarn, also used to distinguish the thickness of yarn.

Popcorn—a group of complete stitches, usually worked in the same place, folded and closed at the top. The number and type of stitches used varies, see page 42.

Puff stitch—a cluster of half double stitches (usually three to five), worked into the same place to make a soft lump.

Rounds—crochet motifs are worked in rounds from the center outwards. Despite the term, they may be square and not circular, see page 34.

Row counter—a small cylindrical device with a dial used to record the number of rows.

Skip—ignore the specified number of crochet stitches of the previous row and work into the next stitch.

Split ring marker—little clips that can be attached to crochet fabric to mark the beginning of a round, or for marking points in a stitch pattern.

Starting chain—the first chain of stitches made for the first round of crochet, made up of the number of chains needed to allow for the height of the stitch being worked, see page 35.

Surface crochet—pattern worked with a crochet hook and yarn onto the surface of a completed crocheted or knitted fabric.

Tunisian crochet—a form of crochet worked with a long hook like a cross between a crochet hook and a knitting needle, producing a fabric like a cross between knitted and woven. It is also sometimes called Afghan crochet and Scottish knitting.

Suppliers

US

Berroco, Inc.
Elmdale Rd.
Uxbridge, MA 01569
Tel: (508) 278-2527

Caron International
P.O. Box 222
Washington, NC 27889
www.caron.com

Coats & Clark
Consumer Services
P.O. Box 12229
Greeneville, SC 29612-0224
Tel: (800) 648-1479
www.coatsandclark.com

Colinette
Distributed by Unique Kolours
28 N. Bacton Hill Road
Malvern, PA 19355
Tel: (610) 644-4885
www.uniquekolours.com

Debbie Bliss, Katia, Sirdar
Distributed by Knitting Fever Inc.
315 Bayview Avenue
Amityville, NY 11701
Tel: (515) 546-3600
www.knittingfever.com

Lion Brand Yarn Co.
34 West 15th St.
New York, NY 10011
Tel: (212) 243-8995

Red Heart® Yarns
Two Lakepointe Plaza
4135 So. Stream Blvd.
Charlotte, NC 28217
www.coatsandclark.com

Rowan/Jaeger
Westminster Fibers, Inc.
3 Northern Boulevard, Suite 3,
Amherst, NH 03031
www.westminsterfibers.
com

Twilleys
Distributed by S.R Ketzer Ltd.
50 Trowers Road
Woodbridge, ONT L4L 7K6
Tel: (905) 856-3447
www.twilleys.co.uk

Canada

Colinette, Debbie Bliss, Jaeger, Katia, Rowan, Sirdar
Distributed by Diamond Yarns
9697 St Laurent
Montreal, QB H3 2N1
Tel: (514) 388-6188
www.diamondyarn.com

Patons
320 Livingstone Avenue South
Listowel, ONT N4W 3H3
Tel: (888) 368-8401
www.patonsyarns.com

Twilleys
S.R Ketzer Ltd.
50 Trowers Road
Woodbridge, ONT L4L 7K6
Tel: (905) 856-3447
www.twilleys.co.uk

Index

Acknowledgments

The Designers

Sue Whiting has been involved in the needlecraft industry for nearly 30 years, at first working for *Fashioncraft*, *Pins & Needles*, and *Family Circle* magazines as well as publishers Marshall Cavendish, Eaglemoss and Fabbri. She now works as a freelance designer mainly for Rowan, Jaeger and Patons, but also for Colinette Yarns, Wendy, Twilleys and Sirdar. She both designs garments and works out technical problems. She has written more than eight books and contributed to many more, not only on crochet but also on knitting, sewing and embroidery. Sue designed the projects on pages 58, 66, 70, 85, 90, 95, 100, 108, 112, 124, 132, 136, 140 and 150.

Luise Roberts was taught at an early age by her mother how to knit and sew. These skills have always been an outlet for her creative talents and she has exhibited as an embroiderer. However, it was with a degree in graphic design and earning a living designing books, in particular several knitting books, that rekindled her interest in crochet. With a new enthusiasm and fresh ideas, she is keen to convey this passion to others. Luise designed the projects on pages 79, 115 and 144.

Sophie Britten is a freelance designer, specializing in crochet and knitwear. She makes specially-commissioned pieces and also teaches crochet and knitting. She has writing several books, including *Fun & Funky Crochet*. Sophie designed the projects on pages 54, 62, 76, 82, 88, 106, 120 and 154.

With thanks also to the makers of some of the projects: Elena Bruce, Ann Casey, Erssie Major, Mrs Palmer and Christine Roberts.